SAILING - SHIP
MODELS

A SELECTION FROM EUROPEAN AND AMERICAN COLLECTIONS
WITH INTRODUCTORY TEXT BY

R. MORTON NANCE

(Revised Edition)

Distributed in U.S.A. by
John de Graff, Inc.
31 East 10th Street
New York 3, N. Y.

1949
HALTON & COMPANY LIMITED
(A Staples Press Company)
Mandeville Place, London   *70 East 45th Street, New York*

FIRST PUBLISHED 1924
SECOND EDITION 1949

Copyright Reserved

Made and printed in England by
STAPLES PRESS LIMITED
at their Bayswater, London, establishment
Colour plate
at their St. Albans, Herts, establishment

CONTENTS

LIST OF PLATES

iii

iv

Plate

v

In the first edition of this book, 1924, the author and publishers, while expressing their great appreciation of the kindness and courtesy of all those who had enabled them to get together the material for it or had permitted the inclusion in it of models owned by them, especially thanked the following:—Mr. G. L. Overton, of the Science Museum, South Kensington; Lieut. Berry, R.N., of the Royal Naval Museum, Greenwich; Colonel H. H. Rogers, Mr. E. E. Kern, Mr. Henry B. Culver and Mr. Clarkson A. Collins jr, all of New York; Mons. Jean Destrem, Conservateur of the Musée de Marine, Paris; Dr. Jules Sottas, Paris; Mr. W. V. Cannenburg, Director of the Netherlands Historical Shipping Museum, Amsterdam; Mr. J. W. Van Nouhuys, Director of the Prins Hendrik Museum, Rotterdam; Rear-Admiral J. Hägg, Superintendent of the State Naval History Collections, Stockholm; Captain Olof Traung, Director of the Maritime Museum, Gothenburg; Mr. C. E. Aagaard, Press Attaché, Royal Danish Legation, London; and Mr. Einar Lexow, Director, Bergens Museum, Bergen. For help with the material for the present edition thanks are due also to Sir Alan H. Moore, Bt., Brigadier C. V. S. Jackson, the late Mr. G. S. Clowes, Mr. F. G. G. Carr, Director of the National Maritime Museum, Greenwich, and Mr. G. P. B. Naish. As before, special thanks are owed to Dr. R. C. Anderson and Mr. G. C. E. Crone for their invaluable help again given with English and Dutch models respectively, of the period 1660–1730.

vi

SAILING-SHIP MODELS

INTRODUCTION

HEN comparing the old seafaring with the new, we must all feel that there, by the loss of satisfaction to the eye, we are made to pay dearly for our material gains. Where from the shore one might once have seen an endless stir of ships and boats of all rigs under sail, each of them showing fresh beauties with every change of position as they tacked hither and thither, trimming their canvas to the mood of the wind, and seeming all, with their heeling, gleaming sides and their cloudy canvas, to have nothing about them that was not as much part of the wind and the sea as the gulls and dolphins that soared or plunged about them; now we have vessels that tack no more, but all go, panting, plodding or racing, straight on their course, with, it would seem, but one idea possessing them—that of removing their factory-like mechanised masses from an element on which they are desecrations, and as hurriedly as possible returning them to the steel-and-concrete dockside landscapes for which alone their most conspicuous features were planned, and in which only do they look quite at home. Even where sails survive as motive power, present-day ideals are so affected by mechanism that the sailing ship has become steamer-like in its proportions, its bowsprit becoming shorter and shorter and its masts growing as like one another as a row of telegraph posts; and the dwindling numbers of smaller sailing vessels that still show us sea-forms suggested by the growth of trees and the needs of hemp and canvas, rather than by the standardised production of metal castings, are but survivals from a vanished age.

Each age in turn has had its own reflection at sea in its shipping, and ours could be no exception, but while we have constant proof that sea adventure is not incompatible with plates, castings, rivets, pipes, cranks and levers, turbines, motors, wireless apparatus and the rest, we all feel that this complex hardware is little suggestive of it, and that the romance of the sea is better expressed by the harmony of line and contour that has always been present in the traditional ship, formed of the kindly and tractable timber, hemp, and canvas of tradition, and designed not to ride roughshod over the elements, but to turn them to her service. Failing to find such symbols of sea-life in being, we are naturally driven to seek them more and more in records of the ships that have gone, and of these the most complete that we have are the models that give us not only the one aspect of a pictured ship, but the whole variety of her lines and curves, and the most intimate acquaintance with all her characteristics.

"Sailing-Ship Model" is a term that may describe things as different from one another as the intricate piece of metal-work that on its reduced scale represents a steel-built, wire-rigged five-master and the crude little wooden thing that by a sailor trick of stick-and-string legerdemain is safe harboured, masts on end, in the shelter of a bottle. Between these two extremes—one of them almost too complex for the plain man's enjoyment, the other too simple even for him—there lies a

I

wide field of pleasure open to him in the handiwork of the ship-modellists of several centuries, craftsmen who, taking upon human hands tasks more fit for the finger-tips of fairies, have made for us so many replicas in miniature of ships of all kinds.

Queens among these are those few that survive in which every detail, down to the last bolt or tree-nail in the hull and the last lashing in the rigging, is exactly as in the original ship, so that to know the model thoroughly is an experience very like that of going over the ship herself. Many are the models that reach this high standard of workmanship as to their hulls, but fewer are so complete as to their rigging, and those that add to these the same perfection of finish in their sails are fewer still. The main reasons for building ship models of this exact sort were practical ones concerned with the ship-builders' art, and their makers had commonly finished their task when the construction of the hull and its decorations were represented. It is probably true that those features of the ship due to the work of the ship-carpenter and ship-carver are best appreciated in such a model, left mastless, only partially planked, and without the final painting and gilding that hide so much tool-work in the finished vessel, and that being so, masts and sails would seem but superfluities; yet in the finest old English ship models we often find masts, spars and rigging, everything in fact save sails, added to a hull that exposes its anatomy unplanked, by way of giving as many facts about the ship as can be shown together.

Next to this class of model, which achieves perfect proportion and is in fact a miniature ship, comes a class that has no such practical origin, but represents merely the sailor's love for his ship, and his desire to perpetuate her features as they seem to him to exist. In the best models of this sort we may find a close approximation to true proportion; but as this is dependent on the eye of the model-maker, who in most cases has worked without even so much as a drawing to guide him, it would scarcely be fair to expect it. This is a ship model for the imaginative mind, perhaps, rather than for the seeker of exact knowledge. Its hull may be "built," after a fashion, but if so its timbers and planking are usually of a very simplified kind and do not imitate those of the ship herself, and more often its construction is even simpler than this, the whole hull being carved from a single block of wood. Where all the work is done by rule of thumb, its finish depending entirely on the hand and eye of the maker, there is room for many degrees of merit in the result, and while in general truth of representation some of these free-hand models are found to run very close to models made from plans, more of them are clumsy and others are even comically grotesque in their misproportion. Age here may, by adding its own glamour and by softening crudities of colouring, count for much of the charm that such rough work possesses.

In those models that have been made to hang aloft, suspended from the roof of a church or hall, however, a certain misproportion, one cannot help feeling, is more or less intuitive, if not intentional, for it is in all countries invariably of the same kind. The underwater portion of the hull, very often marked off by a wave-line of paint in a style sometimes found on ships' boats, especially whale-boats, of their time, is diminished so that the above-water and more characteristic parts may be more conspicuous when seen from below; and that they may not be lost in viewing them at some distance the details of carved work, blocks, and

2

guns, are all magnified. As in a medieval illumination one is prepared to accept the convention of employing different scales in one picture, human interest being represented on one vastly greater than that of castles, ships, or mountains, and kings being twice the size of commoners, so to enjoy the typical church-ship, or even to tolerate it, one must concede to it a similar convention, for to measure it would be as absurd as to compare its figure-head "lion" with a living one at the Zoo. All that one can demand of it (and even that, it must be confessed, it sometimes lacks) is a recognisable likeness to a ship of its time.

Besides these ships of wood and the metal models of metal-built modern ships, we have many ship models made of materials other than those used for the ships themselves. These cannot be said to be as satisfactory to the ship-lover—usually they are too minute to give one anything very intimate—but they may have their fascination as marvellously fine examples of patient craftsmanship, and even as giving details of ship-building and rigging they are not always to be scorned. Some of the finest of these are made of ivory or of bone. The "prisoner-of-war model," built of saved-up beef-bones that have been laboriously sawn into "timbers" and fastened together with brass pins and most delicately hair-rigged at the expense of the maker's pigtail, even when its proportions leave, as they mostly do, much room for bettering, will always appeal to lovers of historical relics. One ivory model at least, the silver-rigged *Norwegian Lion* at Copenhagen (Plate 23), is one of our most valuable records of 17th-century shipping. It probably makes little for permanence that a ship, rigging, sails and all, should be cut out of boxwood, as in some exquisitely fine models, yet it may be of service to have rigging thus rendered in less perishable wire, as it is in some others of our oldest models. Silver in itself, too, is a substance of which, in modern times, some fine sailing-ship models have been made, the gleaming sails having quite a pleasing effect, but unfortunately for our knowledge of the earlier ships that might so well have been perpetuated like these in silver, a silversmith's convention that is not yet abandoned, going far beyond that of the church-ship makers, has always preferred "nefs" or "table-ships" of silver or gold of a kind that never were and never could be, so that there is very little to be got from this source. The finest thing of this kind is perhaps the gold cup or "nef" of 1503 at Nuremberg (Plate 2), inspired by the carrack print by "W.A." (*p.* 33). Copper has been used a good deal for the making of weather-vanes in the form of ships, old as well as new; Dordrecht has two 17th-century vanes, a ship and a hoy, gilded, but presumably of copper, and old Dutch pictures show many such, but here again, where we might so easily have had perfect models of ships, we find for the most part mere conventions, scarcely more useful as increasing our knowledge of actual ships than those glass-blown ships with snaky streamers, whose chief claim to our attention is not that they very closely resemble anything, but that they were so difficult to make, and so terribly easy to break. It would be so natural to imitate some actual ship in these things, and is so impossible to produce by ignoring all truth anything but a deformity that is less pleasing to everyone, that one wonders much why such too-conventional "ships" should still hold the field. It is easier to understand how they originated centuries ago amongst inland craftsmen who had no opportunities of studying the beautiful balance of parts in any real sailing-vessel, and had no "W.A." to copy.

3

As things of joy, apart from all practical ship-building uses and all preciousness of material, ship models have been slow in gaining appreciation, and it is only of late years that their beauty has won them more generally a place that artists have been willing to give them for generations. In studios indeed one has long been accustomed to ship models as a decoration—sometimes painted from, more often enjoyed by their owners simply for their own picturesque qualities—but elsewhere they were rarely seen. "Classical" taste was naturally against them during the 18th century, but the following early nineteenth-century English traveller's description of the Church of St. Nicholas, Boulogne, in days after the "romantic" had displaced the "classical" taste in most things, is worth quoting as showing how little ship models had gained by the change:—"Before it [the tomb of Admiral Brueys] is suspended from the ceiling a model of a man-of-war dressed up with the flags of all nations. Several other ships are suspended in the same manner in different parts of the church, which make a puerile, paltry appearance .... The many paltry paintings, with the tawdry ships before mentioned, render the general view of the inside of the church less imposing than the more chastely adorned church of Calais." This severity is not all intended for the flags, but would certainly include the finest models that could hang there.

Even in the middle of the 18th century it must be admitted that there was some outside appreciation for the more minute work of ship-modellists, at least as "curiosities." In describing the contents of the Royal Museum at Copenhagen, an English traveller, though he is giving but a very brief account of its treasures, finds space to say—"A small man-of-war, in ivory, with silver guns, is a curiosity much admired," referring, of course, to the above-named *Norwegian Lion*. Still more enthusiastic is the following description, written in 1767, of a new-made English model as "a very curious little ship of 64 guns, completely rigged, and but four inches long, executed by an officer in the navy," that was presented to the King, who was most graciously pleased to accept of it, "esteeming it worthy of being placed in his royal cabinet of curiosities." The great attractiveness of this model was apparently due to the number of its component materials, "gold, silver, steel, brass, copper, ebony, ivory, hair, &c., the hull, masts, yards, booms, &c., being ivory, the guns, anchors, blocks, dead-eyes, &c., silver, the 64 guns weighing but fifty grains; the colours, viz., royal standard, admiralty and union flags, the jack and ensign," it is added, "are also ivory, it is executed on a scale of forty feet to one inch." It is to be feared that those who found such tiny models "admirable for their curiosity" were hardly true model-lovers after all, but would have admired even more a thousand copies of the Lord's Prayer written in the space of a threepenny-bit. Kings, as directly interested in things naval, might, without loss of dignity, have such exquisite specimens of ship models in their cabinets, just as our old friend Captain Cuttle might be allowed to adorn his quarters with coarser examples of the art, but without the excuse of being a ship-owner, a sailor, a sea-painter, or a sea-story writer, one would, until quite recent years, have been thought the possessor of barbarous and eccentric tastes who should dare to decorate his room with such things. As time goes on, however, and the beauty of actual sails, already rare, becomes the unknown thing that it seems likely to be, there is no doubt that lovers of beautiful things will be less and less willing to leave these often wonderfully lovely bits of human handiwork unnoticed.

4

Perhaps it is mere prejudice, reaction against the glass-shaded monstrosities of the Victorian drawing-room, that still turns many against any form of decoration, always excepting the water-colour painting, that requires the protection of glass. It is at all events a prejudice that must be lived down by the owner of one of those dainty models of the film-and-spillikin kind that one dares not breathe on, and he will have to be reconciled to this vitreous wall between himself and his "princess in the glass coffin," except on the few occasions when, risking damage to his delicate darling, he lets the air in on her for the purpose of taking exact measurements, a photograph or drawing, or a closer view of some detail beneath the magnifying glass. Little can be done to make the case itself a thing of beauty, for any adornment given to case or stand is apt to be at the expense of the model itself, and the glass-sided box is therefore at its best when least obtrusive. This means that, regarded simply as decoration, such exact and delicate specimens of the modellist's art may have to yield to comparatively coarse and clumsy shippikins, that are hardy enough to brave in the open the risks taken by fine pieces of pottery, painting, wood-carving or statuary, and to survive an occasional expert dusting with a fine brush and bellows. Hung aloft from the roof in church, hall or studio, such a ship seems as free of the land as if it floated; placed, almost as well out of danger, on the top of a high cupboard or tallboy it invites to romantic voyages as no glass-cased ship ever could, and taken down and into the open air the effects of sunlight or moonlight on its sails, the pattern of its shadows, or its reflection in water, even, will give just that admixture of reality and make-believe that is the secret of every aesthetic pleasure, bringing back in another way much of the old glamour that, starting with anything that would float, was able to bring the Indies to a rock-pool on the shore, or the Arctic Regions to a mill-pond. To have made such a model for oneself is ample repayment for the time spent on it; the slow digging out of one's facts, the sacrifice of one's leisure moments, even that monotonous "rattling down" of the shrouds that makes the least exciting part of the work of rigging, weigh as nothing against the comradeship to one's sea-fancies that the finished ship affords as one sets and furls its sails in all possible ways and looks at it from all possible angles. There will be a certain lack, or at least simplification, of detail in such a model, but its happy possessor will be inclined to see even in these deficiencies only another aid to his imagination, and will as easily conjure up the missing touches of its gear as he will raise its elfin crew, or a dream sea on which to set it sailing to El Dorado.

As an inspiration to artists of all kinds, or as a decoration to a room, this super-toy is, perhaps, the ideal ship model, but it is as a work of art in itself, and not for its suggestiveness, nor for its value in a decorative scheme, that the ship-builder's model demands, and is now receiving, attention. Whether it is the superbly carved, high-sterned ship of the 17th century, or whether it evidences the more restrained taste in ship-architecture of another age, it is not merely as a record of past fashions, but as a beautiful bit of handiwork and a miniature copy of the graces of the vanished ship herself that such a model is valued.

In every country the best skill obtainable has always been lavished upon the carved work of ships, and in the 17th century especially no sculptor or painter

5

seems to have thought it beneath his dignity to design allegorical decorations to finish the work of ship-builders. Sometimes, indeed, the greatness of the sculptor was a danger to the ship thus honoured, as when in France Puget grew too exuberantly florid with his rococo high-relief statues and had to be restrained by the firm practical hand of d'Almeras or of Colbert, or, as when given too free a hand on a "ship royal," earlier artists elsewhere added a superfluity of too ornate galleries, embrasures and turrets to what without them had been handsomer ships; for the most part, however, the designers of such work seem to have had an excellent eye for the lines of a ship, and they make the carved work blossom forth from these flowing curves as naturally and inevitably as a flower grows from its stalk or a foam-crest curls from a billow.

It is this justness of design, very largely the result of keeping to conditions imposed by nature, but also the result of profiting by tradition, that makes the beauty of a decorated ship, and we may be very sure that the grander beauty of the hull unadorned was quite appreciated by the artists who have in almost every case added just the final touches of enrichment that give expression to its lines. Thus the ornate ship of 1660 was not merely the ship of 1760, plus a great deal of unnecessary and foppish carving, but the comparatively large amount of decoration had an exact relation to her greater sheer and to her greater height astern, and all of these were diminished together, the difference in decoration between the ship of 1860 and that of 1760 being of exactly the same kind. As there is nothing of man's creation that so closely resembles a living organism as does a sailing-ship, so in a series of ships of different periods we have the closest approach to a scale of evolution in organic life that is made by anything inanimate.

There are two ways of looking at most things, and the evolution of the ship is no exception. We may if we choose see in it a movement towards perfection, at first slow, but latterly very rapid, which culminated with the arrival of the 19th-century clipper ship; the whole scale between *Noah's Ark* and *Cutty Sark* being filled with a series of imperfect ships, less and less clumsy as time advances, but all ineffective attempts at reaching clipper standard. If we adopt this clipper-man's view of ship-evolution we should be prepared to carry it further. The wooden clipper will then but herald the iron ship, and that the steel. The clipper's square-rig sail plan, too, will have to yield to the more advanced arrangement of seven-masted schooners, and in the end all sailing-vessels must be treated as the result of abortive attempts at finding out the "right" (i.e., the most advanced) method of driving a ship through the water by mechanical means. Leaving ships, we should have, on this principle, to condemn all forms of handwriting, including the triumphs of the medieval illuminator's art with the fine flourished hands of his successors, as clumsy strivings after the perfections of the printing-press and the typewriter; all architecture might lead up to the reinforced-concrete skyscraper, or the graphic arts all end in the cinema. This "whatever is, is best" view of evolution in the arts, that for the time ends everywhere in something mechanical, will not please the antiquarian, the artist, and the craftsman, and to others as well it will I believe seem more reasonable to look for many states of "perfection" in the course of ship-evolution, most of which like that of the clipper ship have been

6

reached only to be abandoned in the search for another. We may then take a ship of any given age or country as being a sea expression of the ideals, social and artistic, of that age; often arriving at a finish and poise that may well be called perfection, but ever changing as some newly desired convenience was secured that necessitated a new adjustment of its nicely balanced parts. There must, all through the history of shipping, have been time after time when old sailors, grown used to a settled and "perfect" ship, thought that innovators were ruining the beauty of ships for ever with their newfangles; and in pictures, too, we often find that artists have refused to acknowledge any recent change or addition, preferring ships "as they ought to be."

To look back no farther than to the great sail-less rowing boat of the North, known to us by a specimen dug up at Nydam—its broad keel still showing how it started as a dug-out, its ribs lashed in after the planks were fitted to keel and stems, its bow and stern alike, so that it was always ready to be rowed straight away from the beach, needing nothing in preparation save a re-tying of its reversible rowlocks—one finds that in this a perfection of symmetry had been reached which cannot but have been marred for those who had grown used to it by the addition to it of a mast and sail, and the consequent differentiation in it of bow from stern.

Acquiring poise anew, once the shock of change has passed, we get the noble simplicity of the one-sailed Norse ship of the Viking Age, with its soaring stem and stern-post that carried the curving lines of the sheer straight heavenward, to end in axe-hewn carvings symbolic of all that a ship meant to the men of that day—a sea-steed, a serpent, a dragon. What a destruction of this beauty and imagery it must have seemed when box-like fighting-castles, bad enough when temporarily raised inboard as "stages," far worse, were made to cut across all the gathering together of the curves at bow and stern with permanent platforms and parapets, repeated on a smaller scale even at the masthead, all having no relation to the ship as a ship, but emphasising, on the contrary, a new distinction between seaman and fighter, and putting the latter in all senses higher up.

Yet a new poise was found when "castles" were assimilated, only to be disturbed when seamen found themselves condemned to the indignity of having to steer with a rudder that, instead of being slung on the "steer-board" where as everyone knew a rudder should be, was made by a most lubberly contrivance to hang, as one can fancy them saying, "wagging to and fro on hinges, like any door on land," and that moreover from the stern-post, whereby the clean-ended appearance of the ship was ruined.

It is not long before we arrive at a new type of ship on which any other rudder would look absurd, and the next thing to horrify the "old sailor," who perhaps had taken the innovation of adding trivial-seeming little fore, top and mizen masts and sails more quietly, is the blunt chopping off, astern, of all the graceful gathering-in of the planking that he had been used to, and the substitution for it of the "square-tuck" stern that was characteristic of the 16th century.

In the same way portholes, when first cut for guns, must surely have seemed defacements of a ship's smooth planks; again when through the 17th and 18th

7

centuries the swinging curves of a vessel's sheer, the narrow loftiness of her stern, the profusion of her carved work, and the simplicity of her sail plan, were becoming less with each modification of design, many must have thought sadly of the days in which "ships looked like ships," and when these modifications had at last resulted in the new perfection of a ship as nearly as possible without sheer, without carving, and with batteries emphasised at the expense of form by their straight lines of "magpie" black-and-white paint, still more must have pined for the bright gilding and the shapely yellow topsides of older fleets. This is not merely to say that there have always been grumblers at every new thing, for in every one of these changes there was a real disturbance of an achieved poise, and a destruction, usually with some desirable practical object, of an achieved perfection. Each time, an innovation was to lead to a new type, in itself perhaps as beautiful, sometimes even more beautiful, than the old; but, as first introduced, it was apt to be merely destructive of beauty.

The steady improvement in the ship, regarded merely as a sure, swift, and economical sailing-machine, during this period shows that through the centuries, from the 15th to the 19th, there were certain minds that were not willing to leave things as they found them, yet to the average sailor the average ship of his day has always seemed good enough. If his was not a speedy ship, perhaps it was a dry one. If it refused to sail as near the wind as some others, perhaps it outpaced these when going free, and the main thing was that it should look as a ship ought to look, and behave in the way that a ship should behave, without unduly upsetting the traditions in these things.

As none of us set great value on a ship model as a means of speedy or efficient navigation, but care most that it should satisfy the eye, our own way of regarding these may be much the same, each in its turn being considered by us as a finished expression of the taste of its own age as manifested in the building, decorating and rigging of ships. In the ship of a given period we shall then see something that is all of a piece, not only with its land architecture, but with its costume, and its manners. Thus, in an Elizabethan ship, we shall not only see the expected mixture of Gothic with classical in its strap-work ornament, its balustrades and turrets, but we shall be reminded by its jaunty open gallery and beakhead of the be-ruffled and courtly dandy in trunk-hose that bestrode its deck, and as a final touch the outlicker astern will even repeat for us the effect of the up-tilted rapier that sticks out from beneath his velvet cloak. Similar resemblances between ships of the Restoration period, with their flowing curves and elaborate carving, to cavaliers in feathers, lace and periwigs, to the gabled houses that they lived in, the high-backed chairs that they sat in—even to their flourished handwriting—are obvious enough, and even more is the 18th century written all over the mouldings and pilasters of the stern of a ship of 1750, or early-Victorian culture reflected in a frigate of 1850. If we connect the tubular bridge, tubular coat-sleeves, hats, and trouser-legs, with the tubular funnel and the semi-cylindrical paddle-box of the contemporary steamer and see this rule-and-compass ideal of beauty in simplicity producing a round-countered stern on sailing-ships, or if in contemplating the expansion of feminine crinoline at the expense of human semblance we are reminded of the expansion of canvas in clippers and yachts until the hull becomes relatively a mere straight

8

line on the water, we shall easily go on to find such analogies through all the ages and read the mind of a people in its ships and boats perhaps even better than in its land buildings. When once we begin to do this, such an anachronism as a jib on a Roman galley will seem as poor as a piece of fun as a "bowler" on the brow of Cæsar, and we should no more give the *Santa Maria* a bob-stay than we should portray Columbus in a bob-wig.

In a ship of any given time, as in the life, language, or dress of the community to which it belongs, we find traditional survivals of things past, and prophetic foreshadowing of things to come, so that no one ship can ever be understood if considered apart from all others; yet we find, as we know them better, not only that those of one period have the character that belongs to that period alone, or that there is a certain expression imparted by each rig to the vessel that wears it, but that each ship or boat has an individuality, more or less marked, that is quite its own. Dignity or impudence, innocence or guile, heartiness, cruelty, openness, stealth, determination, flightiness, every quality that is embodied in man, woman, bird, beast or fish, is expressed not only in ship names, but also in ship forms. The rakish pirate schooner and the beamy old Dutch buss of the Dogger Bank, ship for ship, are as contrasted as are their skippers, man for man—the swaggering pirate, lean and swarthy, armed to the teeth; the fisherman, rosy-cheeked and round as a herring-barrel, comfortably smoking his long pipe. The long, low, black-sided clipper, gleaming with gun-muzzles and crowded with canvas; the herring-buss, round-sterned, apple-bowed, and snug, not so much as a bowsprit to dandify her, riding to her nets while the caboose smoke-pipe makes promise of dinner. These are but two extreme types, but they emphasize the point, that a sailing-ship is an expression of human thought and feeling—in fact, a true work of art. And if this is true of a ship, it is no less true of a ship model, made for the pure love of ship form and ship character, and without even the ship-builder's care for any lower consideration of practical utility.

As an art depending on the working together of hand and eye, no doubt the ship-builder's work was at its highest pitch before the invention of saw or plane, for in those days each man needed an artist's skill in the use of axe or adze, and an artist's understanding of his material. Every piece of timber in the ship had been, after due seasoning, picked for its own place, in each was some particular quality of grain or texture that made it the right one, and the dressing-down given it by the well-sharpened tool was to the axe-wielder like the reading of a book, so much was there to be learned about it in the process. We have still existing in the Gokstad and other Viking ships evidence of the wonderful work that was turned out by such old-fashioned, rule-of-thumb methods, and there is no reason to suppose that work as excellent was not turned out by the old Mediterranean builders long before them. When theory and science took over the traditional master ship-builders' work, and invention brought quicker ways of obtaining results, a certain amount of the old instinct for timber-construction and accuracy of eye and hand were lost, but enough of them remain to make common boat-building still a fine thing even to watch, and the older ship models, made by men whose names even are rarely known, but that show these old qualities to the full, though in miniature, are things that almost defy imitation.

9

Most amateur ship-modellists, aware that from the minute accuracy, the exact knowledge, and the endless patience that they demand, such built models are not for them, are content to carve their hulls, acknowledging that were life long enough they would do otherwise. They can make no claim to inherit the ship-builder's art, but theirs, too, is a very ancient craft, not only as imitating the log-hollowing of old, but as following a time-honoured tradition of model-making.

THE tiny, imitative art of ship-modelling, like the great creative arts, had its first beginnings in rites, half magical, half religious, by which man sought to control his fate, or groped his way towards a working theory of the universe, and is probably as old as the art of navigation itself.

The setting afloat of rude models of boats as offerings to the spirits, demons, or gods that control river-currents or sea storms, with hope thereby to avert their attention from the boats themselves, is a rite that one might expect to find practised by the holders of any primitive faith, and one finds survivals of this not only in far parts of the earth, where such little vessels are still launched, but also it may be in places much nearer home, where, as at St. Ives and Polperro and in Sark, Good Friday of all days in the year is one on which every fisher-boy observes a traditional custom of sailing his toy boat, giving a strong suggestion that the custom is a survival from days when a general propitiatory sacrifice of miniature boats heralded the opening of the season of seafaring. It was at Easter too, that egg-shell boats were sailed in North-East Scotland, though in the Isle of Man toy boats were sailed at Pulveel, Rushen, at Christmas.

Such boat offerings may well have been sent on Nile-appeasing voyages down the stream, but in ancient Egypt it is as tomb furniture that we still have ship-models preserved to this day. These again were connected with religious belief,

MODEL FROM TOMB OF MEHENKWETRE

for they were left buried with the owner of the original vessel so that from their lines might be built another fit for his needs in the spirit world. Some of these Egyptian models, although block-carved, are finished with considerable detail, as notably one, perhaps the best, that came from the tomb of Mehenkwetre, Chancellor of Egypt about two thousand years B.C., and is now in the Metropolitan Museum, New York, (p. 11). This shows not only the crew, one steéring, another heaving the lead, but also the mast and sail, the latter with all its rigging, including its boom below with many standing lifts, just as we find these in contemporary wall-paintings and sculptures, the whole giving quite a satisfactory idea of accuracy. It is not in the nature of man to put his best work where it is not to be subjected to the criticism of his living fellow-man, and just as any rough suggestion of a boat was held good enough for fobbing off a boat-wrecking demon, so as provision for the future life of great Egyptians a scamped rough-sketch of a model was commonly made to serve. In such propitiatory or substituted models we may perhaps look for the origin of toy boats, and so of model yachts, but it seems likely that it was rather as votive offerings, open acknowledgments of supernatural aid, made by the christened to be seen of their even-Christians, by the heathen to be seen by fellow-pagans, and displayed in places of worship, that the more complete portraits of ships, the true ancestors of our own ship models, were first made.

Votive junks, highly finished portrait models, are still exposed in Chinese temples, just as in European churches we find hanging church-ships old and new, and a custom that is thus found at the most widely separated points of the Old

World may well be thought to have its roots very deep in the past. In Jutland, whence a church-ship, that of sand-buried Old Skjagen, makes its appearance in literature—coming down from

VOTIVE BOATS OF GOLD, JUTLAND

the roof and sailing away as large as life, in a tale of Hans Christian Andersen's—and where the church-ship is still an institution, a peat-bog has yielded three conventionally shaped votive boats of gold that date back to the first century; but boats and ships of pottery, apparently votive offerings, that go back very much farther than this, have been dug up in Amathus, Cyprus, and Carthage. All through the Middle Ages we have reason to assume that any

VOTIVE SHIPS OF POTTERY, AMATHUS AND CARTHAGE

church attended by seafarers, whether by profession or as pilgrims, would have been likely to have had its *ex voto* ship or ships. Now and then we have an actual record of them, as at Bristol, where in the 15th century the chapel of St. Anne had twenty-seven votive models of wood, to which no monetary value was attached, and five of silver, valued at twenty shillings apiece.

In the Middle Ages, and long after, things that were old were only things to be despised, and worm-eaten models of wood were doubtless pulled down and burnt, and silver models melted down into new shapes, so that the thank-offerings of the living might replace those of the forgotten dead. This alone would account for the total loss of all those one-masted "nefs," "barges," "balingers" and "cogs," with their fore, top, and after "castles," the details of which would have so well eked out those too grudgingly given by conventional seals and yet more conventional monk-made miniatures.

Veneration for relics, other than saintly, is a sentiment far too modern to have saved us any of these, and even without wilful destruction at times of rebuilding or cleaning, models of their kind could not greatly have outlived their makers. To begin with, they were carved from blocks of wood, but slightly lightened as a rule by hollowing, and were of considerable weight, so that it is easy to imagine that a damp church, by rotting ropes, or rusting wires and chains, might have brought disaster to ships themselves as well as to possible worshippers beneath. Even failing such a downfall, their softwood "cage work" and spars, their inferior cordage, and their thinly distemper-painted hulls themselves, were by no means proof against the attacks of time, so that a bare fifty years might thus seem a fair average of endurance for them. It is by an extraordinary chance that we have one left, the Mataró ship (Plate 1), out of all the church-ships of the Middle Ages, and this a built model, with much of her rigging intact.

In those countries that accepted the Reformation one might expect that *ex voto* church-ships, as having been offered in gratitude usually either to Our Lady or to St. Nicholas, the sailor's patron, should have been condemned wholesale as "superstitious," and in England and Scotland this seems to have happened, for from that time we hear practically nothing of such models in these countries; but even this is doubtful, for in Lutheran countries where the church-ship became commemorative rather than votive, as in Catholic countries where votive church-ships are still countenanced, although they remain as a traditional institution, we are no luckier in finding anything earlier than the 16th century, and very little that is as early.

Although they have long since gone to warm the sexton's chimney-corner, lost church-ships may have left traces of their existence in the better-drawn ships of miniaturists and seal-engravers. It was, I am sure, a church-ship that inspired the finest drawing that we have of a 15th-century ship—the *kraeck*, of the Flemish engraver who signs himself "W.A." (*p*. 33). In the first place, this engraver has given full proof in other prints, five of smaller ships, "barges," one of a herring-buss, and one of a line-fishing hooker, that he had slight knowledge of rigging, proving that the carrack's wealth of detail was not drawn from memory. Again, the hull is shown impossibly high out of the water, and is given scanty underwater parts, both suggesting that she was drawn not from a ship but from a church-ship model, a suggestion borne out by the over-large

13

blocks, bored but sheaveless, the twisted-wire fastenings of the lower dead-eyes, and lastly the curious fact that, although otherwise rigged to the final detail, ropes as important to a real ship as the ties and halyards, by which the yards are raised or lowered, are left out. The reason why church-ships should so almost universally have bored blocks only is obvious—sheaves show but little, and would give ten times the work; the same applies to the substitution of a twisted wire for the difficult metal-work detail of the chains, and to a model-maker (who must in these old ships remember to fix his knight-head down below and reeve his halyards through this and the ram-head *before he finally fixes his deck*, if he means to rig ties and halyards at all) it is very clear that the absence of this important gear, so often left out in old church-ships, points to a ship model as original of the picture.

Of three other vessels, two carracks and a galley, in a painting by Carpaccio (Plate 3), there is no question as to their church-ship origin, for they are painted, surrounded by other votive offerings, as features in a church interior. With this hint, it becomes possible to trace back to a similar origin others among Carpaccio's ships, for it is not unusual to find these represented as floating rather unnaturally high out of the water, and with blocks on a scale that makes them too conspicuous. A 16th-century print, representing a philosopher in his study, gives us, with his books and spheres, another little hanging ship

HANGING MODEL IN A PHILOSOPHER'S STUDY

that is an early example of the "lay" model, though hardly different enough from the church-ship to be claimed as a ship-builder's. This is enough to show that artists who were fond of painting shipping subjects might, even in Carpaccio's day, have had little ships of their own, and that they were, even thus early, not peculiar to churches; but with the 16th century we find not pictures only, but several surviving models.

14

If we may judge by appearances alone, the *doyen* of this company is a model from the collection of the late Sir William Van Horne (Plate 7), which is either a church-ship of about 1525 or a forgery of one so skilful as to deserve a high place as a "reconstruction." Unfortunately it comes to us without a pedigree, and worse still after passing through the hands of curio-dealers who were not above tinkering with old models nor even innocent of offering the most bare-faced of "fakes." The rigging, if original, has clearly been tampered with, and its disorder is not necessarily a sign of great age, but it would seem unlikely that a forger should have the knowledge requisite to give the hull of his ship just this combination of high forecastle and narrow, sheering, three-countered poop; round stem and square-tuck stern, and not only to place the guns rightly, and add just the right contemporary touch of herring-bone pattern in the painting, but to render all these characteristic features with exactly the disproportion of above-water detail to underbody that has always distinguished the church-ship. Still more in its favour is its freedom from any attempt at the carving by which ship-model forgers attempt to give interest and value to their productions. It has not even a figure-head, and, speaking as strongly for it as this reticence in decoration, we find under the lower counter two quite un-romantic garderobe vents, of unusual form, but not unlike those of the ship in a window at King's College Chapel, Cambridge, and at all events placed just where they would be in such a ship. The fender-bolts with which it is studded also seem possible enough. If only to invite further criticism, it seems at all events worth while to draw attention to this unvouched-for model, which is certainly not based on any known contemporary painting; for if genuine it is a valuable record, and if proved a "fake" may be as useful a warning.

A church-ship of about 1550 existed until recently at Utrera, Spain, and has been illustrated in *The Mariner's Mirror* (Vol. XV., p. 415) by Dr. R. C. Anderson. An ancient model in the Naval Museum at Venice has there been accepted as representing a Venetian *cocca* or "cog" of the 15th century, as then employed in the Flanders trade. In its present form it is more possible as a ship of the first half of the 16th century, but from the shape of its stern can hardly be earlier, and it has apparently suffered rather drastic "restoration," to which possibly it owes the exaggerated forefoot that seems so little characteristic of ships of its reputed age. Another model at Venice (Plate 9) is a little later in date, being of the fashion of about 1550-1560, but shows a very convincing likeness to the ship-pictures of that date. Although she has been called a *galeone*, she has not the lower beakhead, imitating that of a galley, that marks the 16th-century galleon, but retains the old, ship-style, projecting forecastle of earlier centuries in a but slightly modified form, and should, I think, rather be called a *nave* or ship. A drawing made from this very interesting model by Jal in 1835 shows that her wire rigging has since then been "restored" by someone who has tried to improve on the original arrangement, the braces in particular having now a less correct lead, and bobstays being added, as in the *cocca*. Jal also shows the topsail-yards hoisted higher, as though sails might once have been set on them, and in his time we find that the mizen-yard and the broadside guns were lacking, and that a "ram-head" block was still attached to the ties of the main-yard but twisted round so as to come before the main-mast. The crosses

15

VOTIVE SHIP AT VENICE. JAL, 1835

at the mast-heads (two in Paris's picture of her, *Souvenirs de Marine* III.) are not shown by Jal, and a bulkhead and ladder at the poop are new also; otherwise the little ship is just as she was in 1835, and not very different from what she was when new.

That models of equal accuracy and even fuller detail were by 1550 being made in the Netherlands one might easily guess, but I think we may safely

THREE SHIPS DRAWN BY BRUEGEL FROM A MODEL

16

go further than this, and in two of the shipping plates engraved by Frans Huys, after drawings by Pieter Bruegel the elder, discover carefully-made portraits of one of these. Bruegel in drawing others of his ships may have found church-ships useful, but here we find what looks like proof that he did, for in one plate he gives us a broadside view of a ship with an unusually tall mizen-mast, furled sails, and yards all set a-cock-bill, in what has long been mourning-garb for ships, canted down to starboard on the foremast, to port on the mainmast: and when we find that the next plate gives us three ships, two of which are bow and stern views of this very ship in every detail, down to the exact cock of the yards, remembering the headlong imagination of this artist in his common mood, it is almost impossible not to see in this repetition evidence that it was here restrained by close attention to a model. That an actual ship was not drawn from is strongly suggested by the way in which these three ships are set in the water, as well as by the fact that they are given quite different land-backgrounds. Artists have in later times gained courage to attempt painting moving vessels after practice on the "still-life" of models, and it is not at all unlikely that the skill in ship-painting for which Dutch painters, beginning with Pieter Bruegel, gained so well-earned a fame was in part due to the ease with which they could find church-ships to study.

In 1571 all Christendom was rejoicing over the check given to the Turk at Lepanto, and many must have been the votive galleys or galeasses offered by

LEPANTO VOTIVE GALEASS FROM CRESCENTIO

17

survivors of the fight; but of these nothing remains. One reminder of their existence we do find, though, in a rough woodcut that illustrates Bartolomeo Crescentio's *Nautica Mediterranea* of 1607, and instead of representing a galeass of that date, closely resembles the six galeasses of Venice that took part in the battle of Lepanto. She has not only the semi-circular turret forecastle and ram beak, the guns over the oars, three lateen yards, and Noah's Ark-like deck-cabin aft, of these vessels as pictured, but is obviously drawn straight from a rather roughly made church-ship model that had already had time to get somewhat out of order, the sails having departed from the main and mizen yards and the latter having lost its controlling "orses" and "ostes," so that one need have little hesitation in claiming this as a Lepanto *ex voto*.

As much as Lepanto in Venice, an occasion for thanksgiving and commemoration in England and Holland was the Armada fight of 1588, but of this, too, not a single contemporary church-ship record survives. This is not to say, though, that no ship model was made in honour of the victory, for one, of the little *Francis of Fowey*, of 140 tons and 60 men, a volunteer with the Lord Admiral under command of her owner, John Rashleigh, hung long in the hall of the Rashleigh mansion at Fowey, in Cornwall. Hals, in his rare history of the county, published in 1750, describes this as "a small ship formed by a ship-carpenter, of timber, with masts, sails, ropes, guns and anchors, and figures of men thereon, which is hung up to the roof with an iron chain in their old house in this town, of which those gentlemen have often given me ocular observation." The old house became later the "Ship Inn," so called from the *Francis*, which despite this change, still hung there. Still later it was taken down from its chain, and, as a more fitting position, given place above the last resting-place of John Rashleigh in Fowey Church, with an iron rail to defend it from over-busy fingers. It paid dearly in the end for the dignity of preferment to church-ship rank, for at one of those devastating "restorations" it was cast out and burnt before John Rashleigh's descendants knew of its danger, and of it nothing remains but a uselessly crude little woodcut showing its former position in the church, and the words of description to add to those of Hals, that it was "raised at stem and stern," showing that either its extreme sheer or its raised poop and forecastle distinguished it at once from 19th-century ships.

Another little ship that may well belong to the end of the 16th century is now at the Trinity House at Leith (Plate 11). Its history is a blank, but if a late 16th-century church-ship is not an impossibility in Scotland one might hazard a guess that it celebrated the national thanks for the safe return to Scotland, after long delays caused by witch-raised storms and many months spent in Norway and Denmark, of James VI., with his bride, Anne of Denmark. The date of this, 1590, fits the ship well enough, and the one tradition about her connects her with Mary of Guise, bride of James V., which, though too early, is at least another royal marriage; strongest point of all though, is that she is a great Danish ship, with two turreted galleries, and bears on her taferel the crowned C embracing a 4 that was the monogram of King Christian IV. of Denmark, Anne's brother. From the beginning of his reign this sailor monarch is known to have attracted Scottish ship-builders like Balfour and Sinclair to his yards; but this is not a shipwright's model. On the contrary, it

18

is an extreme example of church-ship exaggeration, and the fact that it has been carefully rigged anew at the beginning of the 18th century hints that it was honoured as a church-ship even at that time. This, too, in Britain, not in Denmark, if such details of the rigging as caps and topsail-sheet blocks witness truly.

Even more incongruously re-rigged, in a caricature of early 19th-century style, is a ship at the Bergen Museum, that for centuries hung in the Church of St. Mary at that place (Plate 21). Bearing an image of Our Lady on its stern, it was probably made especially for this church, to which it is to be restored. Though reputed to be a Hanseatic Bergen-trader, it seems likely to be an emblem of sea-power rather than a portrait, and to show the maker's ideal of the finest possible ship, perhaps again, one of the Danish Navy under Christian IV. With its two roofed-in close-galleries, its turrets and its many guns, it would be, at all events, a great ship of its day (which must be just beyond 1600) and one more adapted for war than trade, even when that might imply fighting one's way to business as part of the venture. With Möller's engraving of a Danish ship of 1600 as a guide, it would be easy to restore to this its old rig.

A model of the end of the 16th century of which we have a little more knowledge is one in the Naval Museum at Madrid (Plates 5 and 6). This is a rather conventional representation of a "ship royal," ideal rather than actual though it is full of good detail, that was made in Flanders and sent by loyal subjects there as a gift to Philip II. of Spain. In 1838, the artist Don Valentin Carderera made a sketch of this ship, then in the Armeria, which Jal reproduces in woodcut form in his *Glossaire Nautique*. He gives but a poor idea of the very elaborate painting that covers the ship, and one band of pattern, that represents appropriately the linked steel "strike-a-lights" of the collar of the Order of the Golden Fleece, is not in his picture. He scarcely does justice, either, to the details of the carving in the delicate foliated scroll-work of the long gallery and the very unshiplike band of carved fretwork enriched with filigree that runs forward from the gallery to the fiddle-head of the beak. An interesting Flemish inscription runs along between the guns of the lower tier, beginning at the port bow:—

"ICK VARRE MET NEPTUNUS EN BOREAS HULPENGHE
TOT DIE HAVEN DAER MI ANKER VALT. ANNO 1593"

"I sail with Neptune and Boreas' help, to that haven where my anchor falls. Anno 1593". Carderera makes the lettering run the wrong way and misreads this date as 1523, a mistake not corrected by Jal, and he was not interested in the rigging, satisfying himself with the masts and tops. The wrong date is easily put right, but the rigging in 1838 must have been in better condition than we now find it, and it is tantalizing to have missed this so narrowly. Although offered to man, mortal though royal, as a symbol of sea-power and no *ex voto*, this ship was perhaps meant to hang with anchors dropped, for in its proportions it follows church-ship conventions; an inscription, even, is not unknown in such models, for one is conspicuous on the white paint beneath a North Frisian church-ship as painted in an interior by Ludwig Dettmann, and the same thing, though much hidden in our view of it, occupies the same place on a 17th-century church-ship that comes from Flensburg (Plate 35).

A church-ship, dated 1603, and in its original condition as to hull, though re-rigged in 1715, and again in 1822, when a crew was added, is in the Germanic

19

National Museum, Nuremberg (Plate 12). This has the open gallery carved from the solid block, but is full of good detail and would thoroughly repay for a third restoration of a more scientific kind.

Of all church-ships the most famous are probably those that hang in the Groote Kerk of St. Bavo at Haarlem (Plates 3 and 13). These commemorate the capture of Damietta in Egypt, the ancient Pelusium (and also the name-place of the fabric "dimity"), after a siege in which William I., Count of Holland, distinguished himself; ended, tradition says, by a Dutch ship that cut the harbour-chain which closed the port, by running at it with a saw-armed prow. This was in the fifth crusade, in 1219 to be exact, but though the clock-chimes— the *Damiaatjes*—that hang in the church tower are said, with what truth I know not, to be one actual thank-offering of Count William, we are not to suppose that the ships are another. They are quite likely, though, to be the latest links in a chain of ships that goes back as far, for a folk-custom of making procession through Haarlem streets in memory of Damietta was kept for centuries by children who, as they marched, carried little ships fixed upon sticks. The present models, a hoy with a lateen mizen, and two full-rigged ships with saw-armed stems, are of the 17th century. The hoy and the larger ship, which is shown in the act of cutting, with its saw, the chain slung between two suspended castles of "Damietta Haven," were made to the order of the Great Guild of Skippers, or Shipmasters, in 1686, and the smaller ship was, one can see, a good deal re-rigged at the same date. She is actually between sixty and seventy years older though, as is shown by her longer beak, her high, narrow poop, her greater sheer, and her open gallery astern. She also has the grating over the waist, the deep round tops, caps open before and topmast lashed to the lower-mast head, with the characteristic heart-shaped dead-eyes and outside chains of this earlier period. This must therefore have been one of the "two models of ships, completely equipped, in memory of that invention of saws under their keels, with which they cut through the chain of booms, which barred the port of Damietta" that John Evelyn saw hanging there in 1641. Huet, the rhyming traveller, who, on his tour to Stockholm, was at Haarlem in 1652, mentions as the most famous sight there, "the ships with saw-like prows, fatal to their Pelusian foes," as his words are Englished. The Dutch naval architect, Witsen, writing in 1671, and a little astray with his history though no doubt following tradition, says, "The ship hangs displayed in the church at Haarlem even to this day which, in 1190, under command of Diederik, seventh Count of Holland,

16th-CENTURY MODEL, FURTTENBACH

opened the harbour at Damietta with a saw at the bottom of the keel, that cut the iron chain by which it was closed." Both Evelyn and Witsen thus mention a saw-armed keel, and not a saw-armed prow, as described by Huet and as seen in the surviving pre-1689 model, as an attribute of at least one of these older ships. Evelyn visualized a wooden boom cut through by a keel driven over it, and Witsen, who knew well enough what ships of 1620 or so were like, seems to have disregarded the saw-prowed survivor, noticed by Huet, to concentrate attention on a saw-keeled ship that he believed to be a contemporary model of 1190. This ship, we may be sure, must have been of considerable antiquity, though, had it survived, we might have had to refuse to give it as he did to 1190, or even to 1219.

Furttenbach's *Architectura Navalis*, 1629, like Crescentio's book, records in its

"DE MAEGT VAN GHENDT," 1672

21

illustrations some models that have ceased to exist. His galleys suggest drawings from an elaborately-finished scale model, but his square-rigged ship is unmistakably copied from a rather clumsy church-ship, with over-heavy spars and blocks. A "Turkish carramuzzal" he gives (*p.* 20) is more interesting than either of these, because, quite unlike a caramoussal, which was a small, moon-sheered high-sterned, and ketch-rigged vessel, it represents a mastless model of a full-rigged ship of about 1550-60, armed with a ram beneath its beak-like projecting forecastle, such as is shown in several contemporary pictures, and also a "saw-like prow" to remind us of Damietta.

With the coming of the middle of the 17th century, we reach many more actual hanging models that have survived, but two in the Town Hall at Bremen, one of about 1625, the other perhaps twenty years later, serve as links between these and the few older models. To the period between 1650 and 1700 belong a number of the models in the Hall of the Guild of Shipmasters at Lübeck, (Plate 39), and one that hangs in the Town Hall at Emden, besides several church-ships in Holland, Denmark, Norway and Sweden, one or two in Breton churches, and at least one Italian church-ship from Genoa. One at Bruges, named "The Virgin of Ghent," and bearing her image on her stern, is remarkable for its unusually good carving, dated 1672, though the ship itself (*p.* 21) is not a very possible one, and has the open galleries and beak design of an earlier date. Although most of these are of the true church-ship type, block-carved, and clumsy as to detail, wavy as to water-line, and scanty beneath it, we begin to find at this time votive and symbolical or commemorative models that are, if not built to scale, at least roughly put together with oversized planking upon a timber frame, and in such models we find often a neatness of workmanship in the rigging that causes the free folk-art of church-ship making to merge into the more exacting art of professional ship-modelling. Yet, through a long succession of church-models, the older methods have survived, as being within the means of the little-skilled, and in Provençal, Norman or Breton churches as in those of Holland, North Germany, Denmark, Norway or Sweden, this crude block-carved model is still the rule. Two notable modern exceptions to this are a fine reconstruction of Niels Juel's ship, *Christianus Quintus*, that was hung as church-ship in a Copenhagen church not very many years since, and a large and perfectly finished model of the R.M.S.P. Company's steamship *Arcadian* that was, in 1923, dedicated as a church-ship at Saint James's Church, Bridge Road, Southampton. More recently a representation of a 16th-century ship was hung at Southampton as a private memorial to a deceased captain of liners. When one thinks of the many great names and events that might be commemorated by the hanging of appropriate ships in British churches and town halls it seems certain that this revival of the old custom will be imitated elsewhere.

It can hardly have been without some hints drawn from the older church-ship of tradition that the first architectural models, examples of true ship-building in miniature, were made. As a theory it is attractive to suppose that such models may first have been made in the form of Mediterranean galleys. Crescentio's *Nautica Mediterranea* gives us, as well as the block-carved galeass of Lepanto, a galley that might well be copied from a built model, and it would be so impossible without actual timber construction to show the lightly built

22

and complicated upperworks of a galley that the attempt might very naturally lead to building such a model from the keel upwards. In time it may be that research will throw more light upon the origins of ship-modelling elsewhere and enable us to see how and where it began, but when first we come across a record of it in England, in 1599, it is as no new thing. This earliest named model was described, by Phineas Pett, its maker, as having been "perfected, and exquisitely set out and rigged." In 1604 Phineas Pett built the *Disdain* for Prince Henry, a navigable ship-yacht so small that it was almost a large scale model, but in 1607 he made, mostly, as he says, with his own hands, a real model for the same prince, "most fairly garnished with carving and painting and placed in a frame, arched, covered, and curtained with crimson tapestry." We could better spare such a mounting than the model it contained, but it at least shows that he knew his work to be worth the best setting that he could devise. In 1634 Phineas Pett, grown too wise perhaps to sacrifice more of his own handiwork, had made under his own direction a little ship for a still younger prince—Charles, then aged four—to disport himself withal, "who entertained it with a great deal of joy." This prince's plaything (Plate 22), was mounted on a "carriage with wheels, resembling the sea," and it may be guessed that its more fragile parts did not long outlive his first taking it in tow. It is interesting to note Phineas Pett's distinction between this "little ship" and his own "models"; the latter word, it is clear, was already appropriated to actual miniatures built from the plans of a proposed or existing ship. Dr. R. C. Anderson, *Mariners' Mirror*, Vol. X., p. 216, draws attention to an English scale-model brought to Sweden by its maker, Francis Sheldon, in 1658, and still preserved at Stockholm. Sheldon, a royalist refugee, gained the position of master-builder at Gothenburg in 1659, helped no doubt by this model, the oldest known English one of its class. His descendants were still in the Swedish service a century later. Pepys tells us, too, how Peter Pett kept up the model-making tradition of his family, and when blamed in 1667 for taking a boat to save his models of ships at the time of the Dutch raid, answered, "he did believe the Dutch would have made more advantage of the models than of the ships, and that the King had had a greater loss thereby."

Pepys mentions elsewhere his own pleasure in a model that he had hung up in his office for his instruction, and in time he acquired a collection of them that was less lucky than his library and, as such, has disappeared. As Duke of York, James II. had his collection, too, that was carefully kept in glass cases, as we learn from the *Travels* of Cosmo III., Grand Duke of Tuscany, 1669, where it is claimed that these models were of his own design. This too is scattered, but the Sergison collection, formed not much later and preserved until recently at Cuckfield, Sussex, is, though no longer in England, still fortunately intact. Model-making in England had the beginning of its literature, in Thomas Miller's *Complete Modellist*, as early as 1664, and the surviving specimens of 17th-century English work at the craft show that something very near to perfection in it had then already been gained here.

If, as we have seen, rigged scale-models of actual ships were being made in England as early as the reign of Elizabeth, we can hardly suppose that they were peculiar to that country. King Christian IV. of Denmark is even said to

23

have been himself a skilled modellist, and little as is yet known of them it becomes likely that by the end of the 16th century similar models were being made elsewhere in Europe. Such models, always of ships of war or of armed merchant ships, would, like Peter Pett's, be kept as precious State secrets until they became obsolete, and then either burnt as rubbish or given as playthings to high-born babies, so that it is not astonishing that records of them should be lacking.

In Holland the earliest models of this kind that survive date from the years between 1650 and 1670, and the Swedish *Amaranthe* model (Plate 26) is of the same date and class. The differences between Dutch, or Scandinavian, and English ship-building at this time were very marked, and even more different were the Dutch and English schools of model-making. The English model, however perfect, stops short when the work of the ship-builder and the rigger are shown in her, much of her framing remains uncovered so that the vital parts of her construction can be seen, and lesser details, colouring, and sails are not given. The Dutch model, perhaps because of the presence then in Holland of so many church-ships to give the example, goes further, giving every detail of the ship when at sea, to her exact painting, even perhaps to her canvas, and if less useful as a guide to the ship-builder concerned with construction, gives that much more to the artist who would know how such a ship looked when sailing. Sometimes, even, by removing the stern, the cabin may also be seen in every detail. This is not to say that no purely constructional models were then made out of England, of course, and some such still exist that date from the 17th century. The oldest surviving Danish model is, like most subsequent Danish naval models, of this class, and represents, unrigged and unfinished, the *Prins Carl*, of 1696.

In France, by 1678, and under the direction of Colbert's wonderful organising genius, a system of model-making was established by which it was intended that the exact form and construction of a vessel of each of five rates should be perpetually fixed. Probably these models, none of which seems to have survived, were not completed with the carved work that would have distinguished any one particular ship of each rating, and as the form of the hull was especially to be perpetuated in them, it is likely that they were unrigged. The miniature vessels of all sorts that made the "flotilla of Versailles," although built on a reduced scale, were perhaps too large to be classed as models, for they seem to have had crews who demonstrated in them the evolutions of fleets, thus bringing the sea to the King's doors. Rigged models, however, can hardly have been a novelty in 1680, when Louis XIV. had a model of a first-rate ship "made, rigged and fitted out in all respects like the ship that was to be built after its pattern." Though this ship no longer exists, the *Royal-Louis* of 1692 (Plate 43) still survives to show how such a model might be finished; this is like the English models in being without sails, but in every other respect is complete down to the last detail of rigging and painting. That the usual contemporary French ship-builder's model may have been left without painting and gilding as well as without sails, though entirely planked and fully rigged, is shown by the wreck of the once very beautiful model of *L'Agréable* of 1695 (Plate 45) decorated by Puget, whose designs for her carved work still exist. In this the colouring is

24

DUTCH CHURCH-SHIP, *CIRCA* 1670-1680. MUSÉE DE MARINE, PARIS

indicated by the use of different woods only, and the beautiful workmanship in what remains of the carving is nowhere concealed. Unfortunately this ship at some period of her history had been allowed to remain exposed to rain, with the result that her timbers had warped badly, making it difficult to restore her without a certain amount of re-building. Her mizen-mast down, her rigging in sad disorder, her guns gone, and despoiled of much of her carved work, I was permitted by the authorities at the Louvre to make some sketches of this model nearly fifty years ago, when she was removed from a lumber-room, along with the battered hulk of an old Dutch church-ship, here illustrated, for that purpose. These two wrecks will perhaps be restored one day. They should both repay for reconstruction by competent hands, for no 17th-century ship model could be undeserving of this, and while the Dutch ship, said to have been Napoleon's spoil of war, has such unusual features as a bench (*banc de quart*) fixed to the poop bulkhead, a defence with two portholes over the half-deck bulkhead, and a second row of cabin lights astern, *L'Agréable* is, both as a scale-model and for its rare detail, of even greater interest.

With the coming of the 18th century we are no longer chronicling the beginnings of ship-modelling. Wherever ships were being built on the grand scale, there models of them were being made, and we still have examples in miniature of most classes of shipping that have sailed the seas since that time. At first it is rare to find any models of merchant-ships, such as were built in private yards for private owners, but though it was not until the 19th century that these were much made except in Holland, we do find a few earlier examples. For models of obsolescent trading vessels of small size, even of ketches and schooners, to say nothing of more unusual types like our own Lancashire schooners, Humber keels and billy-boys, or Severn trows, we may look in vain in most modern museums; local types are better preserved in Holland than anywhere, perhaps,

25

though this is excellently done in some other foreign museums, notably at Altona, but there are, at home as well as abroad, hundreds of traditional "folk-craft," so to call them, local traders or fishing-boats, that making a poor appearance, perhaps, beside the nobility of the sea in the form of ships of war, or even beside its plutocracy in the form of world traders, are yet of an interest to the student of ethnology, and of shipping in its widest sense, that should make it well worth while to preserve them in model form before it is too late. The professional seaman, whatever craft he sailed in, was given to making models of full-rigged ships rather than of any less dignified ship types, and the professional ship-modellist has always been kept busy in reproducing forms either experimental or in the forefront of the movement in contemporary naval architecture. We have now, however, in several countries, but especially in America, with its Ship Model Society, and in England, with its Society for Nautical Research, a large number of skilled amateur ship-modellists, many of them artists, who are all very much alive to the interest of bygone shipping, and although, naturally enough, these are largely fascinated by the possibilities of reconstructing from existing contemporary data the most picturesque and imposing ships of past centuries, some amongst them are taking up this other no less attractive subject of obsolete or obsolescent local types. In such ways, with an increasing number of ship-modellists and diggers out of buried facts, the world may one day have what it is at present far from having—at least one great marine museum where all the efforts made by man towards expressing himself in terms of ship-building might be arranged in model form as in a family tree. If the principle of such an arrangement were adopted even in a comparatively small existing collection, the gaps would become very obvious as one worked backwards in time, while in the largest collection we should find that, taking warships alone, while the past two centuries were over-represented enormously, in earlier periods whole centuries would follow one another with blank after blank; and though the whole wide world might be more or less represented by a number of "folk-craft"—junks, canoes, and catamarans of all kinds—hundreds of equally interesting local types of the home coast would certainly be missing. It is in filling up such gaps with models to represent all that travel and investigation can discover that amateur ship-modellists will render Science their greatest service.

THE DEVELOPMENT OF SQUARE-RIGGED SHIPS

O genealogical tree of ships that could yet be put together would be of that irrefutable kind demanded by
heralds or lawyers; and although much work has been
spent on the evidence, all efforts at tracing their first
parents must as yet be considered as tentative. We are
offered one tempting Father Adam to the whole shipping
race that is not quite as lightly to be dismissed from that
place as *Noah's Ark*, the former favourite. This is the sailing
ship of ancient Egypt. It is beyond dispute that most of the
arts and activities of civilised man had their first beginning
in Egypt, and that in the earlier ages, as far as is yet known, ships were brought
to a higher state of perfection in that country than in any other contemporary
state. It would be difficult to prove beyond the possibility of doubt, however,
that the ideas of making a boat, paddles, rudder, or sails, went either separately
or together out from Egypt all over the world. One primitive form of boat,
that of wicker covered with hide, would seem likely to have originated amongst
people living in a champaign country, where the hunting of large beasts was
varied with fishing, and where timber was scarce; yet the ribs of the framework
of a modern ship may quite reasonably be traced back to the withies of a coracle.
Another primitive form of boat, the hollowed log, must, one would think, have
originated in a land of great trees, such as Egypt never had; and yet this log
is the keel of the same framework. The Egyptian ship evolved, as has clearly
been shown, from a keel-less, rib-less, reed-bundle raft; even as a sea-going
vessel it had neither ribs nor keel, and in its shape still held the contour of the
original reed-bundle—the bowl of an elongated spoon with ends raised and
brought to a point would come very near to it—while its stout planks, though
now firmly fixed edge to edge, still imitated in wood the arrangement of the
parallel bundles of reeds that were lashed together to make the raft. It seems
certain, then, that the dug-out,with the straighter lines that were dictated by
its material, has had its influence in producing the straight-keeled ship of the
modern world, even if we deny that coracles have had any influence in suggesting
its ribbed frame.

Coracles are sufficiently widespread, but to enumerate the countries where
dug-out canoes are used would be to cover almost all the world, for as cheap
and serviceable small craft they survive long after the more difficult art of
ship-building is acquired. A good instance of this was the white-painted dug-out
that I remember seeing years ago carried as a dinghy aboard a barque from
the port of Gefle in Sweden, but the same primitive boat makes a punt for Red
Sea dhows, and shows a persistence elsewhere that is in itself perhaps due to a
momentum acquired in its very long career.

There are two ways of increasing the value of a dug-out. Its want of stability
may be corrected by lashing two together or by adding a dummy boat—an
outrigger; but although almost the whole interest of Pacific Island craft centres
round the varieties of these, we can leave them out of account in treating of the
origins of European shipping, and here the second way, that of increasing

27

its capacity by raising planks upon its sides, becomes most important.

We have, preserved for us by long burial in bog, some actual prehistoric North European dug-outs with plank-heightened sides, and Scandinavian rock-carvings of the Early Bronze Age, as far as they can be trusted, seem to give us a type of war-canoe that is remarkably like that of Uganda. Here the log, hollowed out and raised by a plank along the sides, is prolonged forward into a ram beak at the water-line, while the side-planks are joined at each end to an upright "stem," morticed into the log. The fact that the Uganda boat, so like in other things, is also paddled like the prehistoric Scandinavian one, and even has its bow "stem" adorned with a similar beast's head with horns—the same horns-talisman that 17th-century "Wild Irishmen" bore as an ox-skull on the bows of their sailing curaghs, and that in the modified form of a shark's tail is carried by sailing-ships of to-day at their bowsprit-ends—seems to imply that somehow these two, though so widely separated, derive from a common source, and one that, as far as we can tell, was not Egyptian.

To this source, whatever it may have been, may most naturally be traced the ram beak, most familiar to us in the Greek or Roman galley, but coming to them through Phoenicia from Asia, for this is clearly the pointed end of an original log canoe, still remaining at the water-line, though the log has become a keel, and the single plank has become a whole series of rib-supported planks one over another. Boats from grave mounds in Norway and from Nydam Bog show that development there followed the same line—the dug-out became first a wide, slightly hollowed keel-piece, then a true keel, only hollowed a little right forward where it rose towards the stem, and sometimes given a spur or ram beak just below the water-line, the "skeg" or beard, the name of which is still kept in very similar senses—in English, of a projection at the stern; in Dutch, *schegge*, of one at the bow; in Danish, *skaegget*, of the beak itself. This "skeg" soon ceased to be a ram, however, and the Norse "long-ship," in spite of its oars and its single square sail, was very unlike a Greek or Roman galley; even more different was a Norse round-ship or trader from a Greek or Roman merchant-ship.

These are differences that remained characteristic of Northern and Mediterranean ships for century after century and are not yet entirely obliterated in small craft, so it is worth while to enumerate them, comparing a Roman merchant-ship of the second century A.D. with a Norse trading ship of the tenth. Firstly, the methods of construction were quite different. The Roman ship's stem and stern-post seem to have been covered right up to the forward edge with its planking; the Northern stem and stern-post stood well out. Even more striking, the Roman ship was carvel-built, with planks edge to edge as in the rib-less Egyptian ship and in modern wooden vessels; the Northern ship was clinker-built, with planks that overlapped one another, a method mostly reserved for quite small boats to-day. Used as we are to seeing these building methods alongside of one another, we hardly perhaps realise what an ocean of difference there is between them historically. It is probable too, that, as in modern ships, the frame of a Roman ship was built before being planked over, while the ribs and beams would be put into a Northern ship after the planking was finished and fastened, a survival of which is found in 17th-century

28

Dutch ship-building, where several planks were raised on the keel and "stems" —an under-boat being formed, in fact—before any ribs were put in place. The curves made by the sheer were as different; the Northern ship rising almost if not quite equally fore and aft, while the Roman merchant-ship, as here illustrated, rose far more suddenly astern, repeating the rush-bundle

NORTHERN AND ROMAN MERCHANTMEN

outline of the Egyptian ship from whence she probably derived it. The two rudders, contrasting with the Northern single one, and the projecting beam-ends along her sides came also, it seems likely, from Egypt, where both are found, and the mast, with its masthead block or *calcet* of hardwood for the ties, the square sail with several lifts to the two-spar yard, and the cabin aft may all derive from the same source. The shrouds seen in the Roman ship are new since Ancient Egypt, where they were backstays rather than shrouds, but these, although common to both, have their "eyes" *below* the *calcet* in the Roman ship, and *above* the hounds that serve the same purpose in the Northern one. The Roman sail has a similar square shape, but in all else is quite unlike the Northern one. The latter has (probably) reefs, and a vargord or bowlines; but its yard is without lifts, and comes down when it is taken in, in these things like the North Norwegian fishing-boats of the present day that carry on nearly all of the old Norse traditions of build and rig. The Roman sail is without reefs and without bowlines, while its yard in ordinary weather stays aloft, the sail being brailed up to it with many lines that run from the foot of the sail, up through rings sewn to its seams, to the yard, and thence down, either straight, or in some cases by way of the other side of the sail, to the deck. When these lines are partially hauled on, the sail is diminished, on one side or on both, much as by reefing; when they are hauled right home it is brailed close up, and is then furled by sailors who go out along the yard on a foot-rope—a thing lost for centuries but re-invented when reefing was introduced for topsails in 17th-century ships. The Northern sail is not a mere simplification of this complicated gear, even if, possibly through the leathern sails of the ships of the Venetan-British fleets, it may ultimately derive from the same source; besides this the Roman sail is not solitary, for on a bowsprit-like foremast a little fore-sail, practically a spritsail, is carried, and above the mainsail are set lower

29

and upper "raffee" topsails. On the whole one gets from the Roman vessel an impression of complexity, the result of age-long development and many contacts, and from the Northern vessel one of fresh simplicity that suggests quick growth from a single source.

These two types, Southern and Northern, although belonging to different periods, were good examples for comparison because both were square sailed; had we taken a contemporary Southern ship to compare with our Northern one, the sails, even, would have been of a different shape, for the lateen or lateen-lug had then already displaced the square sail, except, perhaps, as a storm-sail, and had brought its own peculiar gear. No longer bearing the classical Greek or Roman stamp in details, the Southern ship had yet changed little in contour, and the foremast still raked over the bows, the steering was still done with the Latin side-rudders, the yard was still a two-spar one, beam-ends still projected along the sides, the ties of the yard ran through a *calcet* at the mast-head and the eyes of the shrouds encircled the mast beneath it. Such ships seem commonly to have been two-masters, but we find them pictured sometimes with three masts and sometimes with one.

NORTHERN AND SOUTHERN SHIPS, *CIRCA* 1340

Passing over the changes that have taken place in both Southern and Northern ships during the years between, but have left them both true to type, let us take for a second contrast the one-masted Southerner of the sculptured shrine of St. Peter Martyr at Pisa and a typical Northerner of the same date, *circa* 1340, an interesting time because it just precedes the blending of both types in the carrack, and the practical uniformity of square-rig for all Europe that was a speedy result.

Both ships have acquired "castles," fore, after, and top, but these are as unlike as their different origins would lead one to expect. The Southern after-castle is but a modification of the Roman poop, and is really not unlike the poop of the terra-cotta ship from Amathus, of the 6th century B.C. (*p.* 12), while the forecastle, though Roman ships often had a fore-gallery, is in the South a new and rather unusual feature. The top-castle is deep and narrow, and although it is not placed as a "half-top" altogether abaft the masthead *calcet*, as was the more general plan in Mediterranean lateeners throughout the Middle Ages and down to the last days of the galley, its larger part is aft.

30

The eyes of the rigging come beneath this top, and from it a Jacob's-ladder leads to the deck, the shrouds, set up with blocks, being without ratlines. Rising high above the deck round the foot of the mast is usually a series of staves woolded together which form the Southern style partners—the *fogonadura* or "chimney." The yard, a two-spar one, is controlled by ties, that lead through a *calcet*, by a parrel, and at its extremities by *ostes* (vangs) and *orses*, that hold its fore-end down, serving somewhat as the mizen-bowlines on a 17th-century ship's lateen mizen. It is worth while to notice these peculiarities, not only because they always remained typical of the lateen-rigged galley, but because we shall find some of them again in the 15th-century carrack. This Pisa ship shows the Latin side-rudder with its gear, in relief and in fullest detail, putting the projecting beam-ends and retreating stem and stern post beyond doubt in the same way, and in spite of some omissions is, on the whole, the best example of a Mediterranean ship of this period.

The English ship, founded on those in a manuscript at the Bodleian Library

A. HALF-TOP OF 18th-CENTURY GALLEY, LATIN STYLE
B. HALF-TOP OF 14th-CENTURY NORTHERN SHIP

and confirmed by contemporary seals, shows how the separation of types persists—the equal sheer fore and aft is still there, though castles now crown both ends of the ship, and the cutting away of the stern-post to allow of a tiller working over it has brought the after-castle lower than it was when the side-rudder was still used. The clinker-built hull, with projecting stem and stern-post, disguised perhaps under stripes of colour that follow the strakes, is defended by leaf-shaped fender-cleats nailed on to the planking. The shrouds have ratlines, and are probably set up to rings or hearts, invisible inboard. The sail is still square, but has reefs evenly distributed from top to bottom; it still has no lifts, but its bowlines, the ship itself being now too short for them, are set up to a bow-

31

sprit that is given a serrated "bowsprit-comb" beneath, to which the bowlines are adjusted according to the wind. This bowsprit serves as yet no other purpose. The stay is set up around the stem, a vacant space being left in the planking there that serves for this purpose and for the cable as well—the "hawse," or neck, of the ship. Another thing that an earlier, or even a contemporary, ship might have shown would be the Northern "half-top" type of top-castle which is exactly the opposite of the Mediterranean half-top, the hounds for the tie being set in the mast below it, not in a *calcet* above, and the rigging rising above its crosstrees, not below them, while the whole is before, not abaft, the mast. These contrarieties, except that the top is round and encircles the whole mast-head, still exist here, though less evident.

Roughly we may call these two 14th-century ships the father and mother of the 15th-century carrack: now let us look at their offspring.

It will be convenient to take a full-blown carrack that has acquired fore and mizen masts; for one thing because there is conflicting evidence as to which of these masts was first added, although they were seldom both present before the middle of the 15th century, and a one-masted carrack was before either. We are still sadly ignorant of the details of ships before 1400, and hardly know how to reconcile the very varying and often unconvincing pictures of them with written records, or to distinguish one sort of ship from another. We are able to see gradual changes in the shape of "castles," to trace the development of the rudder, and to discover something of the ancient reefing methods, but it is difficult to get much farther. Names refer only to differences of build or size, for all had the single square sail in the North, and yet are known by different names, as ships, cogs, barges, balingers, etc., and some ship names used in the North were given in the Mediterranean to vessels that can have had little but tonnage in common with them; but we do know what a carrack of the middle of the 15th century was like, better perhaps than we know the appearance of a carrack of a century later, and we find that this, though it originated in the Mediterranean as an imitation to some extent of Northern ships, was practically the same thing in all parts of Europe. We have some excellent Italian and French examples that agree, at all events, very closely with the wonderfully detailed Flemish *kraeck* of the engraver who signs his work "W.A." (*p.* 33) giving only slightly less complete renderings of the detail of the rigging, and sometimes adding that of the sails, furled in the Flemish engraving, or of the decks, there hidden.

Great depth was the chief distinction as to build between the 15th-century carrack and other square-rigged sailing ships of her time, for certain of her Southern features had already extended to other types of Northern ship. The fuller bows and much rounder stern, the carvel planking, with its protecting upright skids and lengthwise wales, serving the purpose of the cleats on the clinker-built ship of 1340 in defending it against hoisted weights or wharfside friction, and the greater development of the "castles," are all striking when compared with their counterparts in this earlier ship. Not only are the castles themselves more nearly a part of the ship herself than they were, but they are given, still higher, fighting-platforms that stand above them much as the earliest "castles" or "stages" stood above the deck, and these have tilt-frames over

32

THE *KRAECK* OF "W.A.", *CIRCA* 1450

them upon which awnings, or in battle, nettings, can be stretched. Under the forecastle a noble archway leads to the bitts and to the great, staring, round hawses, beneath which would probably be a trough, the "manger," to catch the water that is drawn in with the cable, or bursts in at them, in spite of the "bucklers" that Carpaccio's Genoese carrack in *St. Ursula's Arrival at Cologne* shows us, allowing it to run back through scuppers into the sea. Along the waist are "cowbridges," gangways of thwartships-laid planking that rise, forward, to meet the forecastle, this raised end, with the arch, making the "cowbridge-head." Similar "cowbridges" or "corridors" run along at each side abaft the main-mast, too, sometimes rising aft to meet the castle at the poop, sometimes coming together to make a complete deck for a few plank's breadth abaft the mast, and showing how the half-deck, like the upper deck amidships, originated as two separate gangways, joined later by a grating and eventually made one deck.

Sometimes Mediterranean carracks are drawn with the projecting beam-ends along the sides that, as we have seen, were a feature of Egyptian vessels, and originated probably in the projecting thwart-ends of some primitive craft in which these, as they often are in such canoes, were lashed to a gunwale. This Southern feature is not a constant one in all carracks, but their rig is invariably Southern in type. The shrouds are without ratlines in so many carrack pictures that the few in which they are represented may be considered as the mistakes of Northern artists; a Jacob's-ladder abaft the mast takes their place on the main-mast only. The eyes of the shrouds make a sort of woolding below the trestle-trees of the top, and they are set up, below, sometimes with Southern-style blocks, sometimes with Northern-style heart-shaped dead-eyes, sometimes with both, dead-eyes being given only to a few aftermost shrouds, and these may be either inside the bulwarks, in Southern style, or on modern-looking channels outside, as in "W.A." 's print. A detail which his view could not show is the Southern-style fascicular partners which rise high around the foot of the main-mast in most other carrack pictures.

The sails are main, fore, and mizen, with a tiny main-topsail, rarely shown set and at first entirely a "top" sail, braced down to the top and sheeted to the top-rim, not to the yard-arms, and occasionally a triangular sail on each side, hoisted to the top-rim and sheeted to the arm and the middle of the main-yard, rather like the Roman "raffees" (*p.* 29); to these a spritsail was not added until near the century's end. The mizen is a lateen, its yard in Southern carracks still given the galley-fashion *mouton*, a rope attached to its lower end, by which it was drawn back and changed over from side to side as required, by being up-ended *before* the mast, but in "W.A." 's *kraeck* the mizen yard is already given a ship-style lift at its upper end, which is in principle exactly the same as those of Elizabethan ships, and changes the mizen *abaft* the mast. These opposite ways of "changing" a lateen yard cause an opposite placing of the "half-top" above it in a 16th-century square-rigged ship to that in a contemporary galley. So that the upper end of the yard shall meet with no obstruction in changing, the former has its half-top *before* the mast, the latter *abaft* it. The carrack usually has no mizen-top, nor half-top even, "W.A." 's being almost alone in this. At first sight the latter might appear to have galley-fashion *ostes* with its ship-

34

CARRACK, *CIRCA* 1550, AFTER BRUEGEL

35

fashion lift; the former are actually two sheets, though, led as far astern as they can go until the "outligger," not yet in fashion, comes in to spread the single sheet farther aft.

Lifts were not used on the main yard of the English ship of 1340. As we have seen, they were foreign to the North; here on the carrack, with their two lower blocks, they are much in evidence, as are also the "martnetts"—ropes branching like a cat-o'-nine-tails, French *martinet*—that gather in the upper corners of the sail in furling it. More tackles, going from blocks at the foot of the sail to others below the yard, and not shown by "W.A.," gather it up into a huge bagful of wind, awkward one would think to handle, especially as the men lay "overthwart the sail-yard" to furl it, without footropes, which had been left behind with the old Roman square sail. Bagginess was a quality desired, though, the sail being given overlapping seams or stitched to bolt-ropes shorter than the cloths in order to gain it, and a middle line of gathering was made as well, that divided the sail into two great wind-bags, or with the two smaller ones of the deep bonnet, laced on to increase its size below, four in all. No wonder that in saying of Sathanas' tail that it was "broader than of a carrike is the sayl," Chaucer should have thought that he had amply stated the matter. A "bowge" drew this great sail in towards the mast by its middle, and bowlines stiffened its weather-leech, but though its braces had pendants, its sheets were still single ropes as in the older Northern ship. Its canvas was for greater strength made "double," that is, with one set of cloths crossing another usually at right angles, though bonnets might be "single," and lateen mizens were always so. These crossed seams are always conspicuous in carrack pictures of the time. The fashion of "doubling" each cloth by folding it down the middle of its length before seaming was prevalent in the next century, as Crescentio tells us.

It has seemed worth while, even in a brief account of ship-evolution, to describe the 15th-century carrack at some length, not only because in it are combined features that belong to two distinct schools of ship-building and rigging, both of which are represented by models in this book, but also because we find in it the origins of many of the features of later ships. "Carrack," as a name, was still retained down to the end of the 18th century, especially for great armed cargo-ships used by the Spanish and Portuguese, but denoted then no difference in rig.

In developing, the three-masted ship-rig, that seems to have begun with the carrack, by the 16th century had grown in some ways less Southern. The shrouds were now always set up with heart-shaped dead-eyes, the chains of which came over the outside edge of the channels, not through holes in them as in "W.A." 's, and were given ratlines, leaving henceforth to galleys only the old Jacob's-ladder. The mizen-lift got the better of the *mouton*, though that galley-style gear remained in use for some time, especially when a second, "bonaventure," mizen was added. Pieter Bruegel, one of whose ships is here shown (*p.* 35), gives mizens of both types. With anything but the smallest of topmasts set before them it was impossible to make the two sheaves of a galley-style *calcet* serve for the ties, and after the middle of the century a thwartships "ass-head" or "moor's-head" cap, over which the ties ran at each side of the topmast, seems to have replaced it on all but English ships. In these latter the old Northern hounds were doubled,

36

so that the ties ran through them below the top, and the cap, made rectangular, with a hole through which the topmast passed, avoiding the need for a lashing, was fitted alongships, a fashion that later, when ties and halyards were replaced by jears, became universal (see illustration *p.* 43, a, b, c). With these new fittings topmasts could easily be struck, and were at once, with their sails, made higher. The hull of the early 16th-century ship or carrack retained the 15th-century shape below, except that the round stern in its first years gave place to a square-tuck and gun-ports were cut in the sides; above, the "castles" grew more consolidated, and the "stern-castle," narrowing aloft, projected aft with counter over counter, overhanging the rudder considerably. Its sail plan had altered as a result of decreasing the mainsail in size and greatly increasing the foresail, and not only were topsails made much bigger, and given to fore, main, and, as lateens, even to mizen masts, but topgallant-sails were sometimes added above them, even studding-sails of some sort were in use, and a spritsail was set flying on the bowsprit. This spar, set to starboard of the stem-head all through the 16th century, and for still longer on English ships, kept its old uses as a means of setting up the bowlines, and as a place for the boarding-grapnel and its chain, which on the Danish *Norwegian Lion*, of the mid-17th century, Plate 23, is still to be seen there. Almost balancing the bowsprit, an "outligger" for the mizen sheet was added astern. From fairly early in the century a boomkin, the French *chique*, was often run out beneath the projecting forecastle, to which the fore tacks were led; with the coming of a lower beakhead this spar was

A PORTUGUESE GALLEON, *CIRCA* 1550, HOEFNAGEL

37

gradually abandoned, the tacks being led to a comb-cleat beneath it, instead.

During the reign of Henry VIII., England, like other countries at the same time, began to experiment with new types of war vessels that might combine the advantages of oared galleys with those of sailing-ships; one of these, the galleon, permanently influenced the form of subsequent armed vessels, to which this name was given, especially by the Spanish, who still had Vera Cruz "galleons" in the 18th century. Built longer, and discarding to some extent the towering "castles" that were ceasing to be of much advantage since improved artillery had lengthened the range of fire, these ships had instead of the projecting forecastle of the medieval ship a straight fighting beak, the origin of the curved, ornamental beak of later days with its figure-head, still called by names equivalent to "galleon" or "galleon figure" in most North European languages. This beak was at first a metal-tipped ram, given either to high-stemmed bows that rose curving in above it like those of a Flemish hulk, or else added below an old-fashioned projecting forecastle as in Furttenbach's model (*p.* 20), but gradually a new type of bow gained ground that stopped short at the level of the beak, the forward part of the shortened forecastle being given a beakhead-bulkhead that corresponded to the cowbridge-head at its after part, and the

ENGLISH SHIP, END OF 16th CENTURY, AFTER RAWLINSON MS.

38

beak itself repeating the under framing alone of the old forecastle. The foremast, always stepped rather far forward, was now placed before the beakhead-bulkhead, this change resulting in what is perhaps the most characteristic feature of the galleon or ship of the end of the 16th century, and the bowsprit was stepped to starboard both of it and of the stem-head.

Another contemporary feature, trivial but almost as characteristic, is the very general use of crowfoot attachments. We already saw the beginning of these in the mizen-lifts and martnetts of "W.A." and Bruegel, but in a ship of near 1600 we have usually a greater complication of them in both mizen-lifts and martnetts, and added to these we have more on the stays, that carrying as yet no sails are made use of for the attachment of braces, bowlines, and the standing parts of halyards, even. The object of a crowfoot is, of course, to spread the strain of a pull over a greater length of rope or spar, and it is still used on the sides of awnings and boat-covers with a similar purpose. The old riggers

CROWFOOT ATTACHMENTS IN A "SHIP ROYAL" OF 1600

seem to have taken great delight in the quaint patterns that they make, for in a "ship royal" they are added beyond what was found useful or necessary in lesser ships, and their names in other languages, meaning "cock's foot," "spider," "goose-foot," give similar expression to this fondness.

The sails of such a ship, though not positive "wind-bags," are still made to bag a good deal, the practice over a century later, even, was to cut the sails the same length as the yard, enough being taken in by the sailmaker in stitching

39

them to the bolt-rope to leave the yard-arms clear of the earings. The theory was that the wind should be held in the sail, and not allowed to escape too quickly at the lee leech. This certainly gave these older ships the *appearance* of making the fullest use of the wind, and in going free these baggy sails may have been as profitable as they were picturesque, even though they might, in sailing on a wind, prove spendthrifts of all such gains. A shallow bonnet, and sometimes a similar sail below that, the "drabler," was laced on at the bottom of the sail much as in the 15th-century carrack; the method of lacing it with eyelet-holes and loops, called "latchets," being exactly that still used for fastening together the wall-cloths of marquees or in those leggings still worn in the country, that lace up in front with eyelets and latchets of the ancient sort. To lace or unlace a bonnet it was necessary to get hold of the sail first, from below, and "lee-fangs," made fast to cringles at the foot of the sail, were used to draw it within reach.

A spritsail, the yard of which ran up and down on a "horse" beneath the bowsprit, stowing alongside the beakhead when furled, was the rule until about the end of the century, when, the "horse" abolished, the spritsail-yard became more permanently fixed out on the bowsprit, with a spritsail-topsail added on a little mast of its own at the bowsprit-end, though this at first only in very great ships. The main-bowlines still, as in 1340 and earlier, led out on the bowsprit, and its use as a place for the boarding-grapnel was not quite abandoned; often, however, a couple of sharp shear-hooks were fitted at the bowsprit-end to match those of the lower yard-arms, and aid in cutting an enemy's rigging.

One of the marked features of the ships of the South had been their galleries astern. "W.A." shows us how a gallery was added abaft the carrack's cabin, but although a stern-gallery is not very uncommon in the middle quarters of the 16th century, it is not until the last quarter that we find it, with quarter-galleries added, in all larger ships, and doubled, as an upper and lower gallery, in "ships royal." At first quite open above, we later find that curved timbers, or sometimes irons, connected its rim with the side of the ship, helping the brackets beneath in the task of supporting it, but serving also as a frame over which an awning could be spread. Just as what were tilt-frames, nettings, and awnings in the carrack developed later into solid structures, so this temporary roof over the gallery led to the making of close-galleries with a permanent roof and a row of glazed lights above what had been the rim level of the old open gallery. Though Monson commends the open quarter-gallery as giving a quick means of giving commands from the cabin to men on deck, its invitation of incendiary missiles was its fatal drawback. At the corners of the open galleries of great ships, and also at prominent parts of these ships themselves, especially at the top of the poop, it was the custom to fix little turrets. A good instance of this is the *Ark Royal*, a picture of which vessel has been used as a base for conjectural models of the *Great Harry*. These were the days of Nonsuch House, and freakish architecture was enjoyed for its own sake, but some at least of these turrets seem also to have been used as lanterns. The church-ship from the Mariakirke at Bergen, Plate 21, even has turret guns pointing from them, but this is an anticipation of modern armament that can hardly be taken serious-

40

ly, and may even be part of the "restoration" from which she has suffered.

The form of these galleries and of their turrets was at first varied with each ship rather than according to its nationality, but as the 17th century wore on, each school of marine architecture settled down into its own peculiar style, for galleries as for beakheads, consoles, port-wreaths, and the rest, and it is easy to distinguish between a Dutch, a French, or an English ship by these alone. As compared with the late 16th-century ship, the mid-17th-century one looked, astern, more compact and at the same time broader, simply as a result of this closing-in of the galleries; the closing of the after gallery, especially, covered up the hollow second counter that had been so noticeable in the older stern, and the carving, which in the older ship had been a comparatively slight touch of decoration, doing little more than lighten the constructive features by removing a little superfluous wood, given a greater continuous surface upon which to expand, blossomed forth in rich relief. A large space on the upper part of the stern was generally kept sacred to the painted or carved name-emblem of the ship, a custom that started in the 16th century. This panel was called in Dutch, *tafereel*, "picture," whence the English word "taferel," and in French, *tutèle*, or *dieu conduit*, from the old custom of naming ships after saints, which so often caused a tutelary image to be put there. At the top of this panel the poop was crowned by a piece of carving that held the cranks of the poop-lanterns, often representing a pair of sea-lions, angels, or cupids, as supporters to a central shield or boss; and a pair of carved figures, called in Dutch *hoek-mannen*, "corner men," and cut on a larger scale than the other carvings, were fixed to the angles above the quarter-galleries at either side of it. Below came the stern windows, and then the old rim of the gallery, called by the Dutch *slingerlijst*, and by them made curved like Cupid's bow. Beneath what had been the gallery was a hollow counter with a tiller-hole and under this in Dutch and other foreign ships a square-tuck stern with its portholes.

As compared with the Dutch stern (*c*) the English one (*d*), suiting its build, remained much more reticently carved, the lines of construction, themselves much straighter, were made to divide most of the surface into small panels, glazed where light was needed, carved or painted elsewhere, and continued down below the stern portholes. With this lighter style of carving the quarter-

STERNS: ROUND, SQUARE-TUCK, AND ENGLISH 17th-CENTURY STYLE

41

pieces and quarter-galleries were, of course, correspondingly light. But the upper part of the poop, though smaller in detail and more compact, was not so very unlike that of a Dutch ship: it is below the counter that the English stern is most different, for while the Dutch one still has the square-tucked *spiegel*, "looking-glass," shape of the 16th century, the English one is made to round up to a transom below the counter somewhat as it did in the *kraeck* of "W.A.", but with the difference that the planking of this "round-tuck" was not, as there and as in the round-sterned Dutch ship of Memlinc (*a*) or its descendant flight or *fluitschip*(*b*), brought round and full to the stern-post as well. This new stern, of course, gave a much cleaner run and improved the ship's sailing qualities, but, like the English capstan, pump, cap, etc., it was not for some time imitated by continental builders, amongst whom the French seem to have been the first to see its merits, and there are still vessels of some size in which the 16th-century square-tuck and even the 15th-century round stern survive, though these are but of local occurrence.

In French ship-building foreign influence was felt in turn from Holland and England, and no very definite national style seems to have been adopted until after the Dutch and English styles were well-established, and with ship-decoration it was the same. When, under the influence of Colbert, the best available native talent was secured for ship-building, this soon resulted also in a French school of ship-carving, of which Toulon was the chief seat. Influenced partly, no doubt, by galley-carving, which gave great scope for figure-work in relief, and partly by the fact that Puget, "the French Michelangelo," was a leading spirit in this school, the decoration of a French stern was made to depart a great deal from traditional forms, and sculptors and practical-minded naval architects were often at variance. The whole was treated as freely as contemporary land architecture would have allowed, the shapes and positions of stern windows being greatly varied; *bouteilles* resembling half-lanterns were substituted for galleries on the quarters, and a wealth of florid design, with much undercutting and a free use of large mythological figures, was lavished upon every part.

Differences as great existed in the carved work of the beakhead and of the topsides generally of the ships of these three nations, and besides this their whole build was usually enough to distinguish them at sight. The Dutch, having shallow water round their coasts, built their vessels with floors very nearly flat, while French and English vessels were sharper and deeper. Two things especially one notices in Dutch-built ships; one is that they have clinker-built "cage-work" and bulkheads, a legacy probably from ships such as Memlinc painted on the St. Ursula casket at Bruges (*a*), where the same clinker-planked "cage-work" is present, another is the very generous supply of fender-bolts with which their comparatively slight timbers are studded, but the spacing of wales and the positions of decks and channels are just as characteristic. It has already been seen that Dutch and other Northern ship-building started in the opposite way to English, French, or Southern building—the planking being started before fitting the ribs; this contrariness went further, for English ships when built were launched stern-first, and Dutch bow-first. The Dutch and Northern builders also launched a ship before completing her upperworks, adding her beak, or building up her stern, while English and Southern practice was to launch a ship completed to the last bit of carving.

In rig, while little national peculiarities existed here and there, as in the matter of caps and lift and sheet blocks, the sail-plan was everywhere much the same; any new thing being so rapidly copied that it is usually difficult to know which country should have the credit of its invention. The early years of the 17th century brought the spritsail-topsail into general use, its advantages having been proved on the "ships royal" to which it was first given. Following close on this came the square mizen-topsail, a handier sail than the old lateen one, which is only found on the largest ships, and there is so seldom shown set that it seems unlikely to have been much used. As with most new things in the way of sails, this square mizen-topsail was given first only to very large ships. A square sail called a "crossjack" seems to have been used occasionally as a storm trysail on the mizen and to have given its name to the cro'jack yard, the *vergue séche*, "bare yard," of the French, to which this topsail was extended below.

a. CALCET
c. ENGLISH CAP
f. DUTCH LIFT BLOCK
b. DUTCH AND FRENCH CAPS IN DEVELOPMENT, 16th TO 18th CENTURY
d. CONTINENTAL TOPSAIL-SHEET BLOCK
e. ENGLISH DITTO
g. RAM-HEAD BLOCK FOR TIES OF LOWER YARD

At first this new sail seems to have been added even when two mizen masts were carried, as, for instance, in pictures of the English *Prince Royal* of 1610, and probably, though its lateen-yard, like the spritsail-yard, is missing, in the Flemish ship at Madrid, Plates 5 and 6; but the bonaventure-mizen soon disappeared, probably helped out of existence by this new sail. This produced a fresh balance in the sail plan—topsails, whose yards were then still only half the length of lower yards, began to grow squarer, topgallant-sails became a more everyday part of every big ship's suit of sails, and the spritsail-topsail was made somewhat bigger. The common 17th-century rig is, in fact, just the common 16th-century rig with the addition of a square sail to top off each extremity, one over the spritsail, one over each topsail, and another over the lateen mizen. This was not of course just so much extra canvas, for with these higher sails came a reduction in relative size of the others, and especially of the courses. With this readjustment came the addition of backstays to help the shrouds. Soon after the middle of

43

the century two other innovations were made: one, the introduction of reefing—at first by one band of reefs at the head of the topsail, to be followed towards the end of the century by a second, and another, that still more altered the appearance of the ship, the addition of triangular stay-sails like those already in long use on hoys (see Plate 61). The latter were probably looked upon as superfluities at first, and are rarely put into models or pictures. Running on light stays of their own, beneath main and mizen and fore and main topmast stays, they did not disturb the old use of stays as attachments for braces and bowlines. The use of stays as attachments for halyards had by this time been given up, and the old crowfoot fittings were now found only for the spritsail-topmast-backstay, or "craneline," that was set up to the fore-stay, for the mizen-topmast-stay that was led branching to the aftermost shroud of the main rigging, and for the mizen-lift. Towards the end of the century jears replaced the old ties of the lower yards, and their lifts, instead of coming in under the top, were led up to the cap.

The beak, all through the 17th century, was growing shorter, thicker, and more recurved; the fore-tacks were, towards 1650, led through holes bored in this instead of through a "comb" beneath it, and later they were led through blocks at the same place. Down to this beak the bowsprit, stepped amidships even in English ships well before 1700, was still very firmly gammoned; for only at the very end of the century do we find a bobstay to give it any additional support, in spite of the fact that the strain of all the other masts comes eventually, by means of stays, upon the bowsprit. Bowsprit-shrouds of the modern kind were still far away, though a sort of "shrouds of the bowsprit"—a gammoning with dead-eyes and ratlines—was for a short time fitted in English ships, as e.g., in the *Soveraigne of the Seas*, Plates 14 and 15.

During the 17th century much exchange of ideas had been going on between the great ship-building nations, and by the coming of the 18th, although in ships there was still diversity enough as to their decoration and build, they were fast growing more alike. French and Spanish builders had arrived at their own compromises between Dutch and English extremes, and the former especially were giving so much attention to the theory and practice of ship-building that they were already beginning to take up the position that they held during most of the century, as the first ship-designers of the world.

In English ships there had always been a wholesome tendency to decorate the construction rather than to construct decoration, and this was carried to a fine point in the years about 1700. The conventional lion had for at least a century been everywhere the favourite figure-head, and it is interesting to see how it is adapted by ship-carvers to the changing beak. The Englishman's lion is now great of head, with a fine full-bottomed wig, his forelegs are bent back at a racking angle and his ribs are extraordinarily prominent, but he fits the curve of the ship's head absolutely, and the same thing happens if a man on horseback is carved there instead. On the magnificent Cuckfield *St. George* (Plate 51), we even find the saint and the dragon brought as beautifully into the right form by making the dragon bend his back into the desired curve. Astern it is the same; though, borrowed from the French, we find an open gallery re-introduced in another form, the poop is outlined with the simplest of curved masses, set

44

out by the ship-builder, and the carved work, however bold, is adapted perfectly to these. Such a rounded poop, resplendent with its bright yellow or gold, must have had an effect like that of a wind-cropped furze-bush in full bloom. This simplification of mass in ship-carving was gained also by the Dutch and the Spanish, each in their own way, but French ship-decorators, and the Danes, deserting the Dutch style in imitation of them, continued much longer to construct decoration astern for the sake of its imposing effect. When we remember that galleys, with their flyaway caryatids and florid sculptures in general, were still in vogue in fashion-making France, we see why through much of the 18th century these ornate vessels were affecting ship-decoration elsewhere. Galleys were used, it is true, in the Baltic also, but there climatic conditions had discouraged superfluous ornament, and they had practically none to impart. The tendency in all countries, France included, was now towards the suppression of carved figures, however, and by the middle of the century, or a little later, we find rococo on the wane and more economical plain mouldings or applied balusters forming the greater part of the decoration of all ships; wreaths around ports, cherubs, and mermaids had gone from them; a figure-head, even, gave place to a shield or a fiddle-head in some, and the flowering-time of the decorated ship was almost over.

CONTINENTAL BOWSPRIT, *CIRCA* 1740

In rig, the most notable innovation, coming in very early in the 18th century, is the jib, set on a new spar, the jib-boom. This spar was at first carried at the side of the bowsprit, and pointing through the spritsail top that, with its mast and sail, survived for some years after the jib came into fashion. Later this top was reduced to a couple of B-shaped projections, "the bees of the bowsprit," and the spritsail-topmast became a mere "jack-staff." In English ships the jib-boom lay on top of the bowsprit and was given a perpendicular cap at the bowsprit-end on which this jack-staff was fixed; in others the jib-boom stayed

45

beside the bowsprit longer, given a cap that was set askew, for the old knee of the spritsail-topmast though made smaller, kept its place as a support for the jack-staff and also for the little netting in which the furled fore-topmast stay-sail lay like a swaddled babe in a hammock. With the loss of the spritsail-topmast the spritsail-topsail found a new home, beneath the jib-boom. Beyond this a separate flying jib-boom with its sail was added later, and below the bowsprit-end a dolphin-striker. Other changes to note are the introduction of a pair of boomkins with blocks for the fore-tacks, thus severing their old connection with the beak (an extension of the single *chique*, that had survived in small beakless vessels), and the addition of reefs to the courses (doing away with bonnets) as well as to the topsails. Studding-sails and royals also became general. The stays of the mainmast were still used, as to the slightest possible extent they are yet, for the attachment of braces, but in the first half of the century these braces were led further aft, and the bowlines were at the same time led

HALF MIZEN, WITH LATEEN YARD RETAINED

further forward, leaving the stays almost clear. Until nearly the middle of the century the mizen in all large ships was still a lateen. Influenced by the example of the hoy's mainsail however, the ship of that time sacrificed the part of that sail lying before the mast, lacing the remainder to the mast, but keeping the lateen yard whole as a help in balancing the peak by its weight, and as an attachment for the mizen-bowlines, still thought indispensable. In smaller ships a gaff mizen like the mainsail of a brigantine was already carried, but the full lateen mizen was still kept in others, being retained by the French long after the English had given it up.

Tops in the early years of the century ceased to be round, their after-part becoming square and thus making a better spread for the topmast shrouds. They had already flattened out until it was difficult to see in them the descend-

46

ants of the bowl-like 16th-century and earlier tops, but they still kept, radiating from their midst, the vestiges of the knees that had supported their high sides, and they continued to keep these after this change of shape, though eventually a grating replaced the old solid platform. Another vestige of old ways was the top-armour, a piece of red cloth or painted canvas that covered a netting held on a stanchion-supported rail at its aft-side. These, of course, balanced the waist-cloths and boarding-nettings, later used as hammock nettings, along the sides of the ship herself, but it is strange, after all this addition of masts and sails, to find in them yet so close a parallel to the "castles" and "top-castle" of the middle ages. The main top, the old "top-castle," was, when an admiral or commodore was aboard, given a further likeness to the poop or "after-castle," by receiving a top-lantern exactly matching the three poop-lanterns. Although the crow-foot was almost forgotten in other uses, the top-crowfoot, introduced late in the 17th century, still rose from a "euphroe," Dutch *juffer*, on the stay beneath, to spread on the top-rim, keeping the foot of a topsail from fretting or hitching there, until the end of the 18th. It was still easy to tell an English- or American-rigged vessel from another by the form of the caps through most of the century. Another little distinction was that in English ships the mizen-topsail braces, until about the middle of the century, still led aft to the peak of the mizen yard; but in others ran forward to the after shroud of the main rigging, crossing one another, so that all the yards could be braced from one side of the ship.

Coming to the 19th century we have, as its chief features, a suppression of the ornamental parts of a ship and an expansion of its sail area. Early in the century the sunk beakhead was exchanged for bows that rose rounded to the upper-deck level, the hollow of the head-rails being filled with a straight head-board. The only other striking change of form was made by the later introduction of the "circular" stern; practical, but unlovely. The removal of the wales, that for most of the 18th century had still emphasised the curves of a ship's sheer, had paved the way for a new method of planking and of painting that laid stress not on the ship but on her armament. The decks, with their guns, had long run almost straight from end to end of the ship, the portholes cutting into the wales where these came in their way, and once these guiding lines were removed the natural curve of the ship ceased to decide the lines of the planking, these following the deck line instead. The ideal of a sheerless ship had been adopted, and to emphasise this new straightness came the fashion of painting the sides black, with a white line along each battery; the portlids being made conspicuous as black on white, the whole thus giving an air of Sabbatical respectability, like that of black frock-coat and top-hat relieved by snowy linen. Small sympathy with mere art was to be expected from those who approved of such a painting, that ignored the form of the ship painted, and decoration was henceforth confined to a little vestigial carved work astern, in which originality was severely checked, and an apology for a scroll beneath the figure-head on which the ship-carver was forced to concentrate his artistic efforts.

Fashions at sea were still, until the middle of the century, set for European merchant-ships chiefly by their navies, and the smart frigates in this new painting were speedily imitated by the warlike East-Indiamen that carried guns,

47

and then by other merchantmen that, carrying none, sported the even less commendable row of "painted ports." This painting of sham ports was actually a revival, partly with the same object of frightening possible enemies, of a custom that had been in vogue with Hanseatic hulks in the 16th century; in its later phases, however, the ports assumed a sloping form that could deceive nobody, and were painted on craft of all sorts, even barges, open seine-boats, and in at least one instance, at Teignmouth, on one-man-power ferry-boats. However false in itself, this "frigate" style of painting, in which a ship was made inconspicuous as compared with her row of guns, real or imaginary, yet had the merit of setting off well the cloud of canvas that she bore; the hull becoming in effect rather like the body that just serves to hold together the glorious wings of a butterfly, and proving how difficult it is to make a sailing-ship other than beautiful.

The sails were now being cut flatter, this leading eventually to the disuse of bowlines, and were bent to a jack-stay at the top of the yard, hiding this from sight as viewed from the lee-side. The boomless mizen with its yard had universally given place to a spanker with gaff and boom early in the century, and during the middle years of it similarly shaped but boomless trysails were commonly added on the main and fore masts. One sail, the old spritsail, was dropped early in the century. Its yard, still found useful as a spreader of rigging, was later divided into two "spritsail gaffs," these in turn surviving on many bows as "whiskers" of iron. Another alteration in rigging was that of bringing the futtock-shrouds in to the mast instead of setting them up to the main rigging.

Although in Europe, except for a few Dutch "flights," and the "pink-ships" and whalers that followed their example, the man-of-war had still been setting the fashion for "frigate-built" merchant-ships, by the middle of the century the Americans, developing the whaler and the trader on lines of their own, had produced a new type, the clipper, that owed little to naval ideals, and was imitated by British builders. Her length and fineness of lines were her own, but her small doubled channels seem to have been invented to leave space for the hoisting of a whaler's many boats. Boat-davits were similarly used on all whalers long before they were adopted in other ships. It was seldom that the clipper, even when English, wore the "painted ports" in flattering imitation of the frigate, being content to look what she was—the fastest, not the best armed, ship that had ever sailed the seas. Now again in such ships a more artistic emphasis was laid on the beauty of their own lines by such slight decoration as they received. An elliptic stern, without cabin lights and with the merest vestige of scroll-work to represent the lost quarter galleries and, forward, a little suggestion of a beak with a figure-head or fiddle-head, sufficed. To have given more would have been as out of place as to cover a racehorse with the trappings of the tilt-yard. For twenty years or more these fine yacht-like ships raced across the seas, piling on not only some "flying kites" that disappeared with them, but also, for economy's sake, splitting up the greater sail areas of their canvas into inner and outer jibs, and upper and lower topsails. Then steam, with the opening of the Suez Canal, took the trade of the British clipper, while iron construction soon put the American wooden ship out of the running. Thus was brought about a new and slower type of merchant-ship—"the clipper clipped." Not the frigate, nor the ocean racer set the fashion now, even for sailing-ships, for those grew more like steamships. Square-bilged, wall-sided, built of iron, and later of steel, given a bridge amidships, with masts and spars of steel tubing, wire-rigged, and with steam donkey-engines, the later 19th-century sailing-ship had little in common with the older save what remained of her canvas. The old clipper, with her foremast set well inboard, had a long bowsprit to balance this, and her mainmast stood well above the others; the steel ship, four or five masted, with most of her masts alike, and with double topgallant-sails almost as big as her double topsails, had lost the traditional pyramidal sail-plan completely and taken one nearly rectangular. Conservatism still assigned to such a ship a modified clipper bow, sometimes even the painted ports of the frigate, and often a wood-carved figure-head. This decoration seems a mere pretence that the ship herself is still of wood, however—a borrowing of timber finery as a poor substitute for the as yet unfound decoration that belongs of right to the steel-built sailing-ship—and quite justly as little of it is added as may serve to satisfy the convention. With auxiliary motor power, and every "labour-saver" that can be thought of, a few last big sailing ships, square-rigged as well as schooners, still hold their own, keeping in spite of its curtailment some of the beauty of sail: we even have some humbler craft, timber-built, timber-sparred, hemp-rigged and still relying wholly on wind and man power, that struggle more or less successfully for existence, but the modern world has on the whole decided against the sailing-ship, great or small.

Such, briefly, are the chief changes in full-rigged ships from the days of "one ship, one sail" up (or down) to those of the five-master, in whose full suit of canvas that original sail—the mainsail—is but as one brick in a wall. To have gone fully into detail, even as it applies to model-making alone, would have filled an enormous book—hull-construction, spars, decks and deck-fittings, kevels, capstans, binnacles and steering-gear, rigging and blocks, sails and rigs, carved work and painting, flags, anchors, guns, each of these would have required a chapter, if not a volume, to do it justice—yet my hope is that this may serve as an introduction not only to the models that follow but to the fascinating study of wooden ships and their sails in times past, a study so neglected that it is still open to everyone to make in it some real discovery.

For sails and wooden ships in the present time the best that can be hoped is that somewhere on this earth they may find a place where they shall be allowed to keep alive their long-descended tradition of sea-craft until some turn of fortune shall cause the world to need them again, and so set them once more on a career of development from form to form. What new shapes they may take is for us quite unimaginable, but if we may judge of their future by their past we may be sure that none of them can fail of beauty.

NOTES ON THE MODELS ILLUSTRATED

Frontispiece. This model is based on the previously described print by "W.A." Note the steep-tub on the quarter, for unsalting meat, part of the shifter's duty being to get into the tub and tread the salt out; the boat, which in being raised or lowered by the tackles passes just where the skids are placed, showing their use as protecting the side; the cargo-port, used long before gun-ports; the crane-line bags or "pokes," their mouths distended by hoops; the bowsprit grapnel; the guns, mounted on the aftercastle, and one in the mizen-top, and the top netting shown on the fore-top, where also is placed a huge dart intended when cast down to pierce the bottom of an attacking galley. The blocks are all without strops, like those of galleys.

Pl. 1. This model of a small trader of *circa* 1450 was until about twenty years ago kept as an *ex voto* in a chapel at Mataró, Catalonia. It is not only unique as a contemporary 15th-century church-ship but is unusual also as a church-ship, in being built and given every detail of structure and finish, even to the caulking and the waterproof coating of the planks as in the actual ship. The intruded stick as "foremast" and some misplacements of rigging show a modern hand, but otherwise she has survived amazingly to confirm or disprove conclusions based on pictures of the time. She seems never to have had a bowsprit. The main-top is built correctly and the blocks are well-made. The great beam across the forecastle, to which the cable seems to have been somehow stoppered, the projecting beam-ends and scuppers, and the general appearance of the ship, have been shown in pictures, but no picture could show the very shallow step of the mizenmast, immediately beneath the half-deck to allow sway for the long tiller beneath. The mast evidently depended for support mainly on its shrouds. A 15th-century Florentine print even shows two additional masts, carrying temporary lateen "studding-sails," set up beside the starboard bulwarks, one just abaft the forecastle cowbridge-head and the other on the fore end of the half-deck, where neither could have had any step, unless one on the deck. This model has been much discussed in *The Mariner's Mirror*, especially Vols. XV., p. 213 and XVII., p. 327.

Pl. 2. This ship's underbody is only a gold cup, but the detachable upper part is close enough to the "W.A." carrack to merit a place among models. The dragon figure-head in "W.A."'s print is exactly the same as the gargoyles given by him to his architectural subjects and not necessarily a close copy: here it is greatly exaggerated in size. Guns are added at the forecastle, which like the aftercastle is far more ornate than "W.A."'s. The cargo-port is copied, chased on the surface, as a hinged door. The rigging is merely set up with toggles to holes in the sides. The craneline-bags have closed mouths and the single top-cranes are set, wrongly, before the tops. The form of the blocks is interesting, so also is the crew in varied dress and pose. As usual in later "nefs," a banquet is in progress on the poop.

Pl. 3. This gives us church-ships, votive and commemorative, *in situ*, the best possible way in which they can be seen. Carpaccio gives us two great ships, or carracks, and a galley, all of *circa* 1500, and thus fairly new when painted. With them are numberless other votive offerings, candles, flags, etc. Well as

Carpaccio shows the decorative value of ship models, this is even more delight-fully seen in the interior of the Groote Kerk at Haarlem, the models of which are described elsewhere. The lantern-like object at the bow of the largest ship is one of the "Castles of Damietta," chained to another on the other side. The middle ship is shown in Plate 13. The hoy, or galiot, is given the lateen mizen that was later exchanged for a gaff sail. Her spritsail is set, and like the English hoy, Plate 61, she has no leeboards.

Pl. 4.   No very precise description of this great ship, whose building "wasted all the woods of Fife," and that when built "cumbered all Scotland to put her to sea," is in existence. Mr. Patterson in making this "reconstruction" was guided by that of Lindesay of Pitscottie, and by some drawings supplied by myself, largely a matter of deduction, since no detailed ship-picture of this date is known, though there are earlier and later drawings which supply the loss to some extent. The forecastle is still of the 15th-century form; the poop is more solid, and over-hangs above the outligger and the square-tuck stern. The spritsail is stowed against the forecastle and the fore-tacks lead to a boomkin, which may have appeared in large vessels by this time. There are two mizens, the smaller of which, the "bonaventure," is here rigged galley-fashion. The gun-ports are a recent addition at this date. Nettings are shown defending the waist and "castles."

Pls. 5 *and* 6.   This is especially valuable for its finely executed detail. The rigging is sadly disordered, but a comparison of its crowfoot work with that of the diagram already given (*p.* 39) will explain most of it. The high, square-rigged main-mizenmast is unique, but a lateen mizen-yard may formerly have been present also, and it is not even sure how much the rigging may have been "restored" in former times. The blocks are mostly unstropped, the dead-eyes heart-shaped, and the caps open before. The decoration is most elaborate, the openwork between the two tiers of guns and along the long, round-ended gallery being very delicate. The hull is covered with bands of painted ornament, one repeating the Burgundy *briquet* badge. The streamers also show the Pillars of Hercules and the "ragged staff" cross of Burgundy, other heraldic emblems of Spanish rule in the Netherlands.

Pl. 7.   This, as already stated, is of doubtful origin, but in many particulars conforms to one's expectations of what a church-ship of *circa* 1525 would be. The absence of gun-ports would suggest, were it not for the shape of the stern, a date still earlier, *cf.* Carpaccio's ships, Plate 3.

Pl. 8.   The drawings of Le Testu have given most of the information needed for the form and rigging of this model, which, as intended to hang, is left solid. Note the half-top on the mizen-mast and the shields on the after sides of the tops. The topsails are still small, and the fore-tacks lead to a boomkin, the *chique*. The martnetts are conspicuous, rising from the lower yards, as in "W.A."'s carrack and in prints after Bruegel.

Pl. 9.   Comparison of this Venetian ship with Jal's drawing brings out, as already noted, some instances of "restoration." The backstays and the over-large rudder may be added to those mentioned.

Pl. 10.   This has more detail than the ship of Plate 8 and shows amongst other things the method of furling topsails that remained usual for over a century (see Plate 79), and the open gallery, with arched timbers leading from it to the ship's side (see note to Plate 74). The spritsail is still furled alongside of the beak. The martnetts now hang in festoons below the furled sails; the ensign-staff is fixed at the corner of the poop, as in Plate 8, and again in Plate 23.

Pl. 11. Adding to the previous description of this model, one may note the decoration of warriors and tritons on the sides and galleries. Open port-lids are represented by crudely cut lions' heads, and a lion forms the figure-head. The carving is thickly covered with paint, but the monogram, "C.4," is plainly visible on the taferel. A curious point in the 18th-century rigging is that the jib-stay is interrupted by being set up separately to and from the spritsail-topmast head, suggesting that the rigger worked from a misunderstood drawing. The mizen is also given a gaff instead of the expected lateen yard.

Pl. 12. On the stern and sails are the dates, 1603, 1715, and 1822, of its making and of later renovations. The latter have not added much beyond a few sails easily distinguished from the old ones, of which some, as notably the main topsail, set as foresail, are misplaced, and the whole requires little more than sorting out to restore it. The caps, open before, topmast, lashed, and heart-shaped dead-eyes, outside the channels, are like those of the Madrid galleon, but the blocks are all stropped. The bowsprit, stepped amidships, has apparently had a spritsail-topmast. The hull, if lacking in underbody, has truthful detail. The aftermost porthole is dropped to the level of the stern ports, cutting through the wale. Besides the chess-tree for the main-tack, there is a lead for the fore-tack in the head-rails and another for the main sheet over the forward edge of the gallery. The cathead is placed at the lowest point of the curve of the head-rails, as in the Madrid ship. Kevels are fixed against the rails at the waist, which has a grating. The anchors are original, the crew, like the poop-lantern, is of 1822, but may be substituted for an older one. The *Francis of Fowey* had a crew, and so has the Nuremberg cup, Plate 2. Crews, even for 18th- and 19th-century models, e.g., Plate 85, are not uncommon. The designs painted on the sails are different on each side, and include: Mercury, a Mermaid, a Pelican, the Sun, the Moon, the arms of the Peller family, and a portrait, presumably of the owner or donor of the ship.

Pl. 13. This is the middle, and oldest, ship of the three shown in Plate 3. The hull is deficient in beam and underbody, but otherwise is faithful to fact. The masts, tops, and open caps are all original, as is also the bowsprit, stepped amidships, but the rigging was evidently overhauled in 1686, the position of the lifts of the lower yards being alone sufficient to show this. The mizen-topsail, topgallant-sail, and spritsail are furled, the other sails are stiffened with wire and painted. The arms of Holland are painted on the taferel, and crossed guns and swords along the quarter; the painting on the poop and gallery is still of 16th-century style. A roughly cut lion forms the figure-head. A grating is shown over the waist. The larger and later model is far more crudely designed than this, though it has, for a church-ship, very good rigging detail.

Pls. 14 *and* 15. In making this, the most ambitious piece of reconstruction yet attempted in any country, Mr. Henry B. Culver has been guided chiefly by the print of the ship by Payne, the stern view of her in a portrait of Peter Pett serving to eke this out, and correcting the imaginary stern that had been given to her by a previous reconstructor. As a "ship royal" this is more elaborately rigged than was usual at the time, and Van Dyck is claimed as the designer of her decorations. The minute way in which every detail of these elaborations is carried out is a strong feature of the model—see *Mariner's Mirror*, 1922, p. 367. Plate 15 shows, from this ship, the characteristic English beakhead of the time in its most ornate form. The comb for the fore-tacks is carved as a serpent. Note the shroud-like gammoning of the bowsprit, shown not only in Payne's print, but also in drawings of English ships by Van de Velde the elder at the Rijks Museum, Amsterdam.

Pls. 16 *and* 17.   Mr. G. C. E. Crone has given us in this model a scientific reconstruction of an 80-ton *jacht* of the Dutch East India Company that is far more perfect in detail than the full-sized reconstruction of 1909, and cannot differ in any important degree from the actual *Halve Maen*, of which no plans exist. Being a small vessel, this has no gallery, no spritsail-topmast, and no round "tops gallant." The mizen half-top is made barrel-shaped, following some old Dutch prints. The spritsail is furled out on the bowsprit, but the fore-tacks still lead to a boomkin, and the bowsprit is set to starboard. The flags, painting, and crew are all equally realistic and correct, making this a most delightfully thorrough contribution to history. See *Mariner's Mirror*, 1922, p. 265.

Pls. 18, 19 *and* 20.   The name *Hollandia* has been suggested for this ship, and also that of *Zeven Provincien*, 1665; she is actually, however, later than either of these ships. The double *slingerlijst* and less lofty stern suggest a date nearer 1680. The hull, as compared with that of an English or even a Swedish ship, is contrived to draw little water, suiting the Dutch shallows. Every detail, even to the interior cabin fittings, was given exactly in this model, the sails of which had been added. The waist-grating has rails, as in the similar model at Ghent, Plate 28; the lion figure-head is typically Dutch of the period, and the beautifully executed stern carvings show the arms of Orange surrounded by the English Order of the Garter.

Pl. 21.   From the keel up to the white bulwarks this is mainly original, though the feminine figure-head is apparently substituted for one more characteristic of the period. The hull is very deficient in beam, as well as in depth. The tutelary Virgin and Child, in high relief, occupy the taferel, but the roof of the lower gallery is continued astern below the figures, a most unusual arrangement. Apart from the galleries and turrets, the most interesting feature is perhaps the row of lion-faces, not on the port-lids, but between them. The after-ports cut into the wales, but are not sunk. The heart-shaped dead-eyes may survive from the old rigging, which probably included two mizens. The foremast is stepped abaft the beakhead-bulkhead, and the bowsprit is amidships; both apparently in their original positions.

Pl. 22.   In *The Mariner's Mirror*, Vol. XXIV, p. 95, I have given what to me seem conclusive reasons for identifying this, the earliest-known English model, with the "little ship" given by Phineas Pett to the four-year-old Prince Charles in 1634 (see *p*. 23). Its "carriage with wheels" probably did not go with it to the Ashmolean Museum, where it was catalogued by Lhuyd in 1685, and it has lost its sails with their yards, as well as the flags and streamers that must once have made it gay, but it still has the original gilding. It is a block model, not built to scale and too small to be effective as a church-ship. The rounded beakhead-bulkhead and varied bulkheads elsewhere are in the true Pett manner. All detachable detail, such as port-lids and even rudder, is omitted. As in the German model, Plate 12, the gallery is carved from the block with an impossibly cut-back upper counter. Single sticks, with metal discs as round-tops, serve as masts, and there are everywhere similar crudities which would be admissable only in a toy, where a general effect of a very pretty little ship was the sole aim. This it would have reached admirably.

Pl. 23.　Finished in 1654 by Jakob Jensen, instructor in ivory-work to King Frederick III. of Denmark, whose monogram is on the main topsail, this represents a ship built at Lübeck in 1653. The gallery is open for a short distance, the ensign-staff is still at a corner of the poop, a grating runs over the waist, the bowsprit is to starboard and a chained grapnel still hangs at its end. The deadeyes are still almost heart-shaped, and the high catheads are like those of contemporary English ships. The rigging details, in silver wire, are of great value; they have been subjected to some ignorant "repair," but this is too obvious to be very misleading.

Pl. 24.　This most picturesque model shows the round stern that characterised the flight or *fluitschip*—a survival of the round stern of the 15th-century Low Country vessels like those of Memlinc or "W.A." An excellent example, allowing for changing fashions, of just such a vessel was engraved by Frans Huys in 1565, after Bruegel. This has on its stern the date 1564, and the establishment of the flight as a type dates from near that time. Flights, built larger and more heavily armed, were used in the Mediterranean and East India trades. This one is probably a Baltic or Norway Trader. Though given a spritsail-topsail she has no mizen topsail, and is very lightly armed. Later flights are shown in Plates 39 and 100.

Pl. 25.　This model was found in a warehouse of the Dutch East India Company at Middelburg, in its present unrestored state. Though an East-Indiaman, the *Prins Willem* differed from contemporary ships of war chiefly in lacking a forecastle, and actually took part in the battle off the Kentish Knock in 1652. The model is remarkable for its fine workmanship, especially notable in the stern carvings, with a figure of William II. of Orange, the arms of Middelburg and Zeeland, and the monogram "V.O.C.M.", meaning "United East India Company, Middelburg (Chamber)." The decks, as is shown by the guns, are made to curve with the wales, those of the gun-room and cabin alone being horizontal. The rigging is not quite contemporary, as is proved by the position of the lifts, the vangs on the mizen-yard and the reef in the mizen-topsail. The top-armings and the half-furled sail give rarely-seen details. The waistboard pierced for musketry, and the clinker "cage-work" are characteristic. The beak is longer, and the sheer greater, in this most graceful vessel than in any ships of the next decade.

Pl. 26.　The original *Amaranthe* model is stored rather than exhibited, at Stockholm, awaiting the building of a Naval Museum there. This is an exact replica made for the museum at Gothenburg, and shows the very minutely exact way in which the original is rigged—see *Mariner's Mirror*, 1913, p. 204. The decks here are nearly horizontal, the ports, as in the Dutch ships that follow, cutting the wales. Dutch influence is very strongly shown throughout.

54

Pl. 27.   An unusually good church-ship, in quite fair proportion except at the head. Since I saw this model, she has been very carefully restored by Mr. J. W. Van Nouhuys, Director of the Prins Hendrik Museum. The restorations, made from contemporary authorities, include all the rigging, the rails of the head and the top of the stern, which had been clumsily renovated in 18th-century taste. The painted wave-line is also a restoration. On the stern is painted her name, with the date 1662, though the ship was built in 1653. She has some points in common with the Dutch church-ship hulk in Paris, but is earlier, and quite different astern.

Pl. 28.   This very beautiful model of a Dutch ship, *circa* 1675, had been used by the Free Shipmasters' Guild of Ghent to carry in procession, and has suffered from misguided efforts to modernize her, made early in the 19th century. She has been claimed as built in 1767, which may refer to earlier alterations. Like the Dutch model in Plates 18, 19 and 20, she is complete even to cabin fittings and has rails to her waist-grating, but she is quite unusual for the period in having the channels, which are original, placed so high and in having had five, instead of the usual three, poop-lanterns. Her fine carving is perfect but for a renewed eagle on the shield astern. Such disfigurements as painted ports, etc., have been obliterated as far as possible for this picture, but an expert restoration of this, proudly claimed as *le plus beau modèle de vaisseau du monde entier*, is badly needed.

Pl. 29.   This is the first of a series of fine English models, several of which are here shown in a similar position, making it easy to note the gradual change in ship-building style during the next half-century. Here the great height astern, apparently serving only for parade, is very noticeable, linking this to earlier ships. The contrast between this and the contemporary Dutch vessels in shape and decoration is a striking one.

Pl. 30.   This very beautiful model of a richly decorated English ship has recently been re-rigged in contemporary style. As compared with the last ship, Plate 29, the stern is much lower, though still high. Both ships have an elaborate entry-port on the larboard side, and their quarter-galleries and other decorations are similar.

Pl. 31.   This fine piece of reconstruction shows how much Danish ship-builders had by this time got away from Dutch models. The present ship shows French rather than other influence in the form and decoration of the stern, with a return to open galleries of the type that became usual in the 18th century. The port-lids painted with the national *Dannebrog* colours will be seen again in later Danish ships.

Pl. 32.   The *Royal James* shows the long rake forward of her time (all the better perhaps because of the missing head-rails), balanced by the considerable sheer, and the high stern. The English Royal Yacht gives more cabin-room than usual; the after ports are blocked up, with carved flowers within the port-wreath.

Pl. 33.   Below is shown, on a larger scale, the typical head and decoration of the time—the figures along the bulkhead, the port-wreaths and the painted trophies, the equestrian figure-head and many caryatids. The cathead has the star decoration so often seen there later. The three lower wales are unusual. As we have seen, *jacht* in Dutch could be used of trading ships like the *Half Moon*, and not only of such ornate craft of state as is shown above, that were hoys in rig but miniature ships in build. The term came into English from Holland, with the type, after the middle of the 17th century. Though sometimes a ketch, sometimes ship-rigged, the yacht remained in England a vessel of state and pleasure, but in Norway and Denmark the *jagt* is a little square-tucked coaster. Like *chasse marée* and "ketch," the name implies a vessel used for "chasing."

Pl. 34. *La Réale* shows the Latin-type galley in all her glory. Beautiful as galleys were, it is impossible to forget how all this gorgeousness of gilded carving, painting, tilts, and banners, only made more conspicuous the misery of their rowers, condemned innocents and kidnapped redskins, under Colbert's relentless rule mixed with captives and criminals and chained to their benches.

Pl. 35. As compared with the *Christianus Quintus*, this Danish ship is far less unlike a Dutch one. The name-board with *Urania* is 19th-century, as are also the gallows-bitts before the main mast, the sails, and most of the rigging. The inscription below records a personal name only, but is interesting as such. The growing size of the false stem, making here one convex curve from keel to lion, is a late 17th-century trait, exaggerated in the church-ships, Plates 41 and 42. A date, 1719, on the stern, seems too late to be original.

Pl. 36. This very beautiful model was formerly at Ghent. The upper part of the stern had been lost, and that of the *Hollandia*, which ship the model otherwise resembles, has been substituted by Mr. G. C. E. Crone for the incongruous work that replaced it. The rigging is also a restoration. Ships of this class were the largest then built in Holland.

Pl. 37. This is the only known model of a 17th-century Dutch three-decker. But few of them were built, this one probably representing the *West Friesland*. Though not built to scale the model is good in detail, and Dr. Anderson, who has presented it to the Scheepvaart Museum, has been as careful in giving her the Dutch rig of her time as in rigging the many fine English models restored by him. The ship is practically a built-up two-decker, giving her a very high beak-head-bulkhead. Note, in this and other foreign ships, the higher position of the channels as compared with their place in English ones.

Pl. 38. Another superb English model, showing in many ways the gradual settling down into 18th-century form. The skids at the waist are a new feature.

Pl. 39. This shows how closely the Dutch fashions were copied in Lübeck in 1690, the date on the stern of this flight, a larger and later specimen of the type shown in Plate 24. In England the "coal-cat," later becoming the collier-brig, the "pink," and the whaler, showed copies almost as close of the Dutch round-sterned fly-boats and flights.

Pl. 40. Though given an incongruous rudder and a clumsy head, this, for a church-ship, is unusually well proportioned. A gold swan is carved on the stern, and the name is apparently that of an actual ship. The guns are small rather than large, but the blocks are, as usual, oversized. The rigging, though badly disarranged, is original. The spritsail-yard has wandered to the top of the bow-sprit, and the mizen-yard is missing. The running rigging is sadly messed up, and she was always given a short allowance of shrouds.

Pl. 41. A grotesque, but correctly detailed church-ship. The port-lids are left out to make room for the enormous guns. The rigging is original, and almost untouched, but the hoisted yards suggest that sails were there formerly.

Invisible here, on the stern is the lion of Norway, with its curved-handled axe.

Pl. 42. Though Genoese, this church-ship is remarkably like the last in some ways, but is more completely rigged. Although, as in the Bergen ship, the lower yards are fitted with jears, the caps are still open before, and the top-masts lashed, as in ships of the beginning of the century. Note the elaborate setting up of the fore-topmast stay. Dutch rather than French influence is shown in the decorations.

Pl. 43. This is the most magnificent specimen of 17th-century French model-making, and almost the only one that exists. It is complete in every detail except those of the sails, showing many typically French features. The short bowsprit and mizen-mast increase the unlikeness to either English or Dutch ships. The stern carvings are rich in the extreme, with open galleries of the later style. The upper ports are arched and lidless, and four skids are present at the waist.

Pl. 44. This shows the yacht in her hoy rig, *cf.* Plate 61. The model originally had the unusual feature of sails, the boltropes of which alone remained when Dr. Anderson undertook her restoration. The yards are not well seen in the photograph, but she carried a square topsail like that in Plate 81.

Pl. 45. The cause of the dilapidation of this beautiful wreck has been already stated. Finished in great detail, she is somewhat like the *Royal-Louis*; she has arched ports at the poop only, however, and her bowsprit and mizen-mast are less unusually proportioned.

Pl. 46. A fine specimen of English ship-carving. The stern is still divided by continuous lines of brackets and pilasters, but now has an open gallery added. The panels between the carved work are painted, the monogram, "W.M.R.," and the portraits of William and Mary being conspicuous. The channels of the period are well seen here.

Pl. 47. The lower picture shows the ship of Plate 46 in another aspect. An entry-port is now placed on the larboard side also. The upper picture shows how the same sort of work was adapted to a smaller ship. The port-wreaths and dotted star decoration, seen in the yachts of *circa* 1670, still held their popularity.

Pl. 48. A typical English ship of her class. The bowsprit is here given no round-top.

Pl. 49. The lower picture shows the unusual detail of support for "waist-cloths" fore and aft, though not in the waist from which they first took their name. The Venetian trading galeass is without her three lateen-rigged masts, her oars, and her rudder, and her bow and stern both imitate current ship fashions, but she enables one to imagine the beauty of the galeasses that came to England and Flanders in the 15th century "wel ladene wyth thynges of complacence."

Pl. 50. Seen from above, this shows a little of the diagonally arranged benches with the *coursie* running down the middle. The guns are all forward under the *rambade*. The poop, in older galleys a mere tilt-frame, is here solid. The mizen-mast is also a new feature, added only in the largest galleys. The *calcet* mast-head blocks, and shroudless rigging set up with tackles, *couladou*, in Latin style, are clearly seen.

Pls. 51, 52 *and* 53. The finest of the wonderful Cuckfield collection of

57

models, this *St. George* is finished in fullest detail, and is a perfect record of contemporary rigging. The hull shows a further movement towards 18th-century ideals, but is still as splendidly decorated as ever. The fish-davit is rigged out ready to fish the anchor, and the smallest details are everywhere perfectly rendered. The mizen-topmast stay still branches on to the main shrouds, and the mizen-stay is given an unusual crowfoot tackle like that of the mizen-lift. In Plate 52 we have a closer view of the decks and quarter. The back of the carved taferel is here itself carved. The entry-port, with its balustrade, comes right on to the channel as in earlier ships. Plate 51 gives us the finely composed figurehead of St. George and the Dragon, and such details as the stowing of the anchors, the "horse in the head" with its dead-eyes and lanyard, and the fore-tack, led in now at a hole in the middle rail. Particularly interesting is the main-top, too, with all its surroundings.

Pl. 54.   This shows various foreign influences in which the French predominate. Round ports are still given to the half-deck. The rigging is unfinished, and there are no guns, but there is much good detail. The date of the model is likely to be nearer to 1720 than to 1691.

Pl. 55.   Here the 18th century asserts itself still more strongly than in previous English ships. The sheer is markedly less, and the lessened height aft corresponds. The channels are lifted to a position above the middle tier of ports, at last imitating foreign example. The upper ports are without wreaths, and the carved work greatly reduced.

Pl. 56.   This ship may be compared with that in Plate 48. Several anomalies in the rigging here shown have now been corrected.

Pls. 57 *and* 58.   The intimate view of the *Britannia's* decks aft—not completely planked, so as to show the construction—shows how far the enrichment of a great ship of 1700 was carried. With it all, the back of the carved timber of the taferel is left like the back of a carved chair or mirror of the time, its pierced parts simply chamfered off. The way in which the curves of the staircase rails are made to interplay with those of the ship's rail is very pleasing. Plate 58 shows the stern, still keeping much of the 17th-century English convention, but given two open galleries, the lower of which is extended to the quarter. The fighting cavaliers as design are more successful than the rather distorted figures at the corners. The royal arms and the three interlaced anchors of the Admiralty ornament the galleries, and a lion's head still, as in earlier ships, forms the rudder-head. Below is the bow with its equestrian head. The bitts and timberheads are all given carved heads. Those at each side of the bowsprit are still perpetuated in the modern use of the term "knighthead."

Pls. 59 *and* 60.   Plate 59 shows the great variety of stern design that could be given to ships of the English fleet at this transitional time. The arcading on the counter of the middle one, repeated at her beakhead-bulkhead, is almost Elizabethan, while above it are pilasters suggestive of the later 18th century. The carving everywhere is rather an ornamentation of a space left plain by the ship-designer than part of an ornamentally designed ship. In Plate 60 the quarter-deck guns alone have wreaths, and though enrichment lingers plain mouldings are on the way while the sheer and forward rake grow less.

58

Pl. 61.   This shows the general appearance and rig of one of the commonest types of its period. Two 18th-century hoys turned into lightships seem to be the only contemporary models of these vessels—English translations of Dutch galliots like that at Haarlem, Plate 3. Originating as spritsail craft, these were given a "half-sprit" or gaff, a rig adopted for yachts like that of Plate 44. The round stern of the hoy, like that of the "pink," was given a very projecting "lute" aft, which resembled the stern of a galley more than that of the Dutch original.

Pl. 62.   Two interesting smaller vessels. The top one was probably rigged as a snow, and is rather yacht-like in her proportions. The lower ship is larger but slightly too small for a man-of-war of her class, and is perhaps a yacht.

Pls. 63 *and* 64.   These ships, built, one on the establishment of 1706, the other on that of 1719, illustrate well the trend in ship-building. Port-wreaths are denied the latter; the head reaches the maximum of contraction, and the carving is diminished. The second is a notably detailed and well-rigged model. Note the top-armings and main-top lantern.

Pl. 65.   The now almost circular stern has greatly changed since the 17th century. The lowering and broadening astern has gone on as in English ships, but with other results, the curve of the *slingerlijst* still asserting itself, though the taferel, like the English one, has become a mere edging at the top of the stern. Over the tiller-hole are carved the arms of Batavia, the seat of Dutch government in the East Indies, a sword *in pale* within a wreath. The details of carving and the poop-lantern are still of 17th-century style. The *Padmos* at Rotterdam, and other models at Dordrecht, show similar sterns.

Pl. 66.   The lower ship, very handsome of body if less decorated, shows the new joined wales of Plate 68. One is perhaps better able to judge of the beauty of this ship as a ship because the framing is not shown below. She has the dimensions of 1719, but is a very late member of her class. The upper ship shows a slight return to older fashions. She is given oar-ports, although a 60-gun ship. A sea-horse takes the place of the usual "lion."

Pls. 67 *and* 68.   These models, both remarkably fine specimens of the art, represent the same ship in her "re-built" form of 1719. They differ, however, in one important item; the lower wales being separate in the rigged model and joined together in the other. This is interesting as dating the introduction of the joined wales in English ships, which seems likely to have taken place between the first planning and the final building of this ship. The skids are not fitted to the Greenwich model and there are other minor points of difference. The tops now ceased to be round; a break with very old tradition. The rigging (Plate 67) is modern, but approximately correct.

Pls. 69 *and* 70.   The addition of sails makes this the most complete English model of so early a date. The hull is now definitely of the 18th-century form, and the decoration is only a slightly more ornate version of the standard 18th-century mode. The so-called "flying jib" on its jib-boom is now introduced, though not with the approval of Wm. Sutherland, who says of it that it is "a sail of good service to draw the ship forward, but very prejudicial to the wear of the ship . . . 'Tis used with a boom or small mast extended at the extremes of the bowsprit." Sutherland, *Shipbuilder's Assistant*, also named studding sails as in common use, but we as yet find no stunsail-booms fitted to models. The sails

59

of this *Royal George* allow us to see the reefs, as yet but few, in the topsails. In the stern we already have the small gallery balusters and larger windows of later ships and the taferel is cut across with a fourth row of lights, while the old continuous lines of pilasters and brackets have quite gone.

Pl. 71. The lower wales are still separate, but all ports are square, and there is little carved work. The poles are those from which flags were flown at the launching ceremony.

Pl. 72. The lead of the fore-braces, farther back on the stay, if of 1742, is a very early example. Probably the rigging is nearer 1750 in date. The mizen is of the "brigantine" pattern, first introduced in ship-rig for smaller ships such as this. Hammock-nettings are shown. The topsails are close-reefed, and the top-gallant-sails sent down and stowed in the rigging. The current severity of taste has affected the carved work, and the sheer is slight.

Pl. 73. To the details of deck-arrangement and display given before, this adds the striped sails with their *orses, ostes*, and other running rigging. The *rambade* is here, as in another Maltese galley at the Science Museum, given an embrasured defence like the medieval "castles." Note the grapnels as anchors, the very long beak, and aft of the *apostis* on which the oars rest the curved accommodation-ladder that is usually raised when not in use.

Pl. 74. Here the stern is less circular than in *Den Ary*, Plate 65. The clinker-work above survives and the quarter-gallery is given a series of carved timbers that are elongated descendants of those seen above the open gallery in Plate 10. These survive on the gallery roof and appear again, in Plate 90, on a still later Dutch ship. The sails of this East-Indiaman show us our first example of the cut-down mizen, with yard kept whole, and also of studding sails. The spritsail-topmast has gone, but the spritsail-topsail is set on the jib-boom. Royals and a mizen-topgallantsail are shown, and three reefs to the topsails. The waist-cloth and waist-board pierced with musket-holes survive from the 17th century.

Pl. 75. All ports square, joined lower wales and a "classical" stiffness in the quarter-galleries characterise this fine model. The spritsail-topmast is still of importance and has its top. The entry-port is now beneath the fore-end of the main-channel, in this differing from its position in the original draught of this ship.

Pl. 76. Lent to a marine painter who was told to "do what he liked with it," this model was fired at and returned in its present condition—an example of the small appreciation given by one artist to the work of another, perhaps better skilled, in a different art. The result is at least picturesque and the wreck above emphasises the beautiful and characteristically French work of her decorations. The uppermost ports, square below, are arched above in the older style. The rigging is contemporary, and beautifully executed.

Pl. 77. As compared with earlier ships, one notices the disappearance of wooden statuary. The quarter gallery is surmounted by a clock-headed survival of the half-turrets of former days, but ends below in the same spiral that we have seen in English ships, beginning as a fish-tail in Plate 63. Stunsail-booms are fitted, but no royals or mizen-topgallantsail is carried, and the mizen is a lateen.

Pl. 78. Although Dutch, the decorations fore and aft are here French in type. The model is not built to an exact scale, but has much good detail.

60

Pl. 79.   This model, though finely finished and decorated, is not built to scale. She is impossibly dumpy as compared with the Swedish scale-model in Plate 83 that represents a similar ship. The stowing of the sails, the topsails still "farthelled" as in the late 16th century, is excellently shown. The trophy-painted topsides are no longer clinker-worked, and the lion at the head and the galleries astern follow French models.

Pl. 80.   The general trend of sea-fashions affects all countries similarly. Thus in this and Plate 76 we see joined lower wales, as in the earlier English ships. Here the carved work astern is entirely Spanish in style, though the shapes that it decorates are suggested by French design. The upper-deck ports are lidless. The realistic way in which the ship is "laid up" is very interesting. The rounded fronts of the topmast crosstrees are relics of the round top there. The knee of the old spritsail-topmast is still kept in its place, the bowsprit cap being set askew.

Pl. 81.   The Dutch yacht by 1750 has changed little from that of 1650 except in the carved work. Leeboards were not wanted in the deeper-built English yacht and hoy, otherwise there is little difference between this and those in Plates 44 and 61. The Dutch gave the un-hoylike peak-halyards as seen here to 17th-century yachts also. The scarfed topmast is a medieval survival, and the stem-head still curves back as in the 15th-century fishing boats drawn by "W.A.," the stay being set up to it by a lanyard passing through holes in it, a fashion imitated not only in the English yacht and hoy but in later cutters. The wooden fenders are a Dutch contrivance, but rough log fenders of the same sort are still in temporary use in every harbour.

Pl. 82.   One of the finest of French models, this is wonderfully complete in detail. The rigging and sails are a fine example of restoration, in which a flying jib, however, seems too early. The stern decorations are here completely *rococo*, with little trace of older conventions.

Pl. 83.   This is not unlike the Dutch East-Indiaman, Plate 79, in all but proportions. The shifting of the fore braces has by this time practically cleared the stays, giving a more modern appearance to the rigging.

Pl. 84.   This shows, very beautifully, the current taste in decoration. The classical sculptures and the painted trophies and scroll-work survive from the 17th century, but the pilasters and balusters and the shell ornament over the light-ports on the quarter are quite of the period. The lower wales are separated.

Pl. 85.   A block carved model with a wooden crew aboard, and with contemporary rigging and sails.

Pl. 86.   Here the mizen is a boomless trysail, much like that of the old hoy or yacht. The main and mizen channels are in one. The caps are made English-fashion, and the bowsprit cap is no longer set askew.

Pl. 87.   This frigate has oar-ports, so low that some of them cut the joined lower wales. The lateen, or lug, mizen-topsail yard is unique, but a dolphin-striker on the bowsprit suggests a later date for at least part of the rigging.

Pl. 88.   Models of such smaller craft are proportionately rare. The mainmast of such a schooner would perhaps have had a square topsail also, for one commonly sees this in contemporary pictures. The little window on the quarter was in some such vessels a mere dummy—the quarter-badge—put there to satisfy those who missed the quarter-gallery of bigger ships. The window originated in yachts, as in Plates 33, 44 and 81, long before.

Pl. 89.   1775 is too early for the precise rig of this reconstructed armed lugger. Lescallier gives no lugger in his *Vocabulaire*, 1777, and in his *Gréement des Vaisseaux*, 1791, gives one with squarer sails and without a mizen topsail. The rig originated in the English Channel, deriving from that of square-sailed fishing vessels of the "Biscay shallop" type. Armed luggers like this were used as despatch boats, revenue cruisers, smugglers, and privateers. The fore and main topmasts are set abaft the masthead, and the rigging is composed of runners and tackles instead of shrouds. The cut of the sails is probably incorrect for any period.

Pl. 90.   This is a beautifully rigged model with every detail, to sails and painting, carefully worked out. She still has the characteristic Dutch quarter-gallery, and is given oar-ports.

Pl. 91.   Built in Holland, *circa* 1660, this was long the fastest ship afloat, easily making 16 knots. Chapman, the author of *Architectura Mercatoria Navalis* in whose English parentage we may take pride, lived as a child on board this ship when she was moored at Gothenburg, and a drawing of her then made by him still exists. From this, and plans in the book named above, this model was made, showing the ship, rebuilt, as Chapman knew her. The round ports were perhaps original: she is given oar-ports as well.

Pl. 92.   Interesting as showing the persistence of the Latin tradition, even after galleys were given up, in a fighting ship. Some beautiful chebec models at the Musée de Marine, Paris, show that in France also they were valued. The shrouds here, as in modern Mediterranean lateeners, are not like the galley's *sarties*, but rigged *à colonne*, i.e., with runners and tackles. The projection aft is not unlike the "lute" of an English pink or hoy. The beak imitates that of a galley and oar-ports are fitted between the gun-ports. The type has changed little since the 17th century.

Pl. 93.   The head is typically French, the forward rake being less than in English ships. A new thing here, and in Plate 82, is the doubled tack, the fore-tacks leading to blocks on boomkins. Bruegel's presumable model shows double tacks, but this is not confirmed elsewhere, and single tacks, made tapering, have hitherto been the rule. Inner and outer jibs are shown, perhaps too early. The half-mizen, with its lateen yard, is well seen, and also the boat hanging from the tackles. Davits as yet are confined to whale-ships.

Pl. 94.   As in the English ship, Plate 97, the upper wales are joined. No dolphin-striker is fitted, and the mizen still has a yard. The high-placed channels would at once distinguish this from an English ship.

Pl. 95.   A specimen of Chapman's designs—an attempt to combine shallow draught with great speed. Crankness was often a defect of this inventive designer's experimental ships. There is a canvas waist-cloth amidships, which when raised allows of oars being used. The schooner rig with square topsails on both masts was common well into the 19th century.

Pl. 96.   A reconstruction, from plans and paintings, of a snow; a vessel like a brig, but having a square mainsail, and behind it a trysail with a slender mast of its own. The hull derives from the beakless flights, cats, and hulks of long before, but the stern is not made round after the Dutch fashion.

62

Pl. 97.   The upper wales are here joined as well as the lower, but keep a considerable sheer. The rigging is not contemporary, but illustrates such then novelties as the gaff mizen and the dolphin-striker.

Pl. 98.   Interesting as being probably the oldest existing model made in America. Though not markedly unlike an English ship of her class, she already has a hint of the breaking away from European tradition that was to produce types like the American whaler, frigate, and clipper ship.

Pl. 99.   This has been thought to have been made by a prisoner of war in 1779, but the rig will scarcely allow of it; 1812 seems more likely if it is an American war-prisoner's work. It is a fine specimen of the unprofessional model. The curve of the rails of the head is at last destroyed here with a straight rail, and we see a mizen-topgallantsail for the first time set.

Pl. 100.   The *bootschip,* "boatship," is a descendant of the old flight, Plates 24 and 39. These vessels were sometimes built round up to the top of the stern, making them into ship-rigged galliots. Dutch whalers were of this build, with just such little windows in the stern cheeks. The windlass is seen just abaft the foremast, which is further forward than in modern ships. Old fashions survive in the "ass-head" caps with ties still running over them to "ram-head" blocks. The sail plan is still that of fifty years before, and the spritsail-topmast knee is seen on the bowsprit. Such round-sterned Dutch vessels were still extant after the middle of the 19th century.

Pl. 101.   Another snow-rigged vessel; one of the earliest of American models. Unlike the Danish snow, this has a boom to its trysail. The rigging, e.g., the spritsail-yard set over the bowsprit as a spreader, is not all original.

Pl. 102.   The "pinkship" of the Baltic, like the English pinks, was originally round-sterned in imitation of Dutch fashions. The stern here with its davits is more like the square-tuck still seen on Danish coasters. The "pinkship" is distinguished from the "frigate-ship" especially by its lack of a mizen topgallantsail. Here the other topgallants and the royals are rigged in polacca style, both coming down together when furled.

Pl. 103.   This shows the latest 18th-century fashions. The stem is less raking and the beakhead lighter and smaller. The decoration is slight, but there is still considerable sheer, though the wales have grown inconspicuous. A spanker boom is a conspicuous new feature. There is also now a flying jib-boom, at first a separate spar.

Pl. 104.   An example of the large class of bone "prisoner's models," this one is very highly finished; the crowfoot to the mizen gaff is rather typical of their involved work. Another "extra" is the "sprit-topgallantsail." The double dolphin-striker of the time is well seen here. The black bands on the hull are not usual on such bone models. Boats are added; one hanging at davits astern.

Pl. 105.   Here as in Plate 103 the wales are less conspicuous, and the channels are all at one level. Ironwork has come into use for nettings. There is no dolphin-striker, and a mizen-yard is still carried.

Pl. 106.   French and English ships were changing together. The lower poop, and the mizen channels in line with the others, distinguish this from the *Hero* of Plate 107. The sails, hammocks, and awnings are all shown drying, and one of the ship's boats with sails is also seen. The spritsail and spritsail-topsail are still carried.

Pl. 107.   The lessened rake of the stern and the very slight sheer show early signs of the 19th century; the waist, however, is still open, and the beakhead, except for the straightened upper rail, is of the old pattern. Boat-davits are fitted astern only.

Pl. 108.   A block model, not carved to scale, but interesting as showing the American frigate type—a very much more powerful ship than a frigate of Europe. The beakhead-bulkhead has now disappeared, the bows being brought up round behind the beak, and the head-rails, topped with a head-board, carrying the straightness of the rest of the hull right forward.

Pl. 109.   The davits on the quarter, if original, would put this ship farther on. The quarter gallery and the head, with the marked sheer aft, seem early features, and so does the short jib-boom.

Pl. 110.   Bomb-ketches had at their origin been round-sterned and Dutch-built; hence the French name *galiote à bombes*. This one carried 2 mortars and 8 guns. The rig derives from small hooker-like coasters, and had been used in England for yachts also. It is practically that of a foremastless ship.

Pl. 111.   This shows, below, the finer lines introduced by Sir W. Symonds. The rounded bow, covered waist, and straight head-board are new since the *Hero*, Plate 107; so are the boat-davits on the quarters, and the trysail gaffs on the fore and main masts. The spritsail-topsail is seen no more, and the spritsail itself is rarely set. The cradle for launching is seen alongside.

Pl. 112.   A "Symondite" brig, this has the sharper build introduced by Sir W. Symonds; as here rigged it shows the "spritsail gaffs" on the bowsprit. The similar training brigs, useful as giving instruction in square rig on a small two-masted vessel, were the last representatives of sail in the British Navy.

Pl. 113.   A rough, disproportionate block model, but of an interesting type. The American whaler has travelled a long way from the flight-built Dutch *walvischvaarder* that set the fashion for 18th-century English and other whalers. Another whaler model at New Bedford is enormous, being built half the size of the original. It was on whalers that the old wide channels were first abandoned as being in the way of the boats. This model is without channels; those of the large model are narrow and protected by skids. The fiddle-head takes the place of a sculpture, and plainness is the prevailing note. The flying jib-boom is still a separate spar. The double dolphin-striker serves as "spritsail gaffs" as well.

Pl. 114.   Showing a reluctance of French builders to adopt the new sea-fashions, in build and rig *L'Hercule* resembles the *Hero*, Plate 107, rather than the *Vanguard*, Plate 111, keeping the square beakhead-bulkhead and carved head-rails, and also the deep waist. She has no quarter davits, and keeps her spritsail-topsail yard and top crowfeet, given up in the English ship.

Pl. 115.   This is still a "frigate-ship" rather than a true "clipper," but shows fine lines with a good deal of American influence. The narrow channels are placed high, the foremast has travelled back from the bows, a "monkey-gaff" is carried and outriggers spread the backstays at the topmast crosstrees. No sail is as yet carried on the cro'jack yard. The fore braces now lead down to the sides; no longer to the main stay.

Pl. 116.   The early cutter, like this one, was usually clinker-built. Her rig derives in part from that of the hoy, Plate 61, but she is given a running bowsprit and a "brigantine" mainsail that lowers and has a boom. The stay in older cutters is always set up to the stemhead as in the hoy; the dead-eye being turned in "cutter-stay-fashion," leaving room for the sail to run down close to the stem when lowered. Very fast boats, these had to contend with cutters and luggers of the "Smuggling Service" that were often faster still, and as well armed.

Pl. 117.   Something of a freak when built, this fine McKay clipper has the four-masted barque rig that became typical of the big merchant ship. Her double topsails are of the original pattern, the lower topsail having two reefs and being larger than the upper one. She has the typical sheering bows of the American clipper, and the masts are more gracefully varied in height than in her successors. The deck-houses, somewhat resembling contemporary railway-carriages, are conspicuous recent additions to the sailing-ship.

Pl. 118.   The double topsails are now of the modern kind, the lower topsail yard being fixed at the cap. The mizen-topsail is still single, but a sail would be carried on the cro'jack yard. The spanker is fitted snow-fashion, with a little snow mast, and a monkey-gaff carries the "Stars and Stripes." The deck-houses and most other details of the hull, including the double channels, are just as they remained in American ships of the "eighties" and "nineties" and set the fashions to a great extent for all sailing merchant-ships. English clippers were by no means a mere imitation of these American ships, but the type, originating in America, is perhaps best represented by a ship such as this.

Pl. 119.   The hull is of wood, but with iron beams. The nearly upright stem, flat sides, turtle-back poop, and round stern also suggest iron construction and steam. The bowsprit and the spars generally are somewhat stumpy as compared with those of a clipper, though many of her features are derived from such ships.

Pl. 120.   This steel four-masted barque, Masefield's "*California* huge, as slow as time," represents almost if not the very last word in square rig. Double topgallant yards were later carried as well as double topsail yards, saving trouble but adding to the monotonous effect given by the repetition of detail on each mast. The hull keeps some of the sheer of the clipper, but its extreme length makes the stump bowsprit seem even shorter than it is. Ventilators aft, anchor davits forward, and a donkey-engine amidships all suggest steam; but this ship has not adopted the auxiliary steam or motor propulsion that we find in some that are still newer. One of the latest "novelties" in square-rig, the use of parallel brails running through rings on the sail, is a belated revival of Roman custom, see *p.* 29. The present tendency is towards a simplified schooner rig, however, and auxiliary motor power which, to judge by the effect of steam, is likely to end in complete victory of mechanism over sails, cheapness being gained by saving on man-power what is spent on fuel.

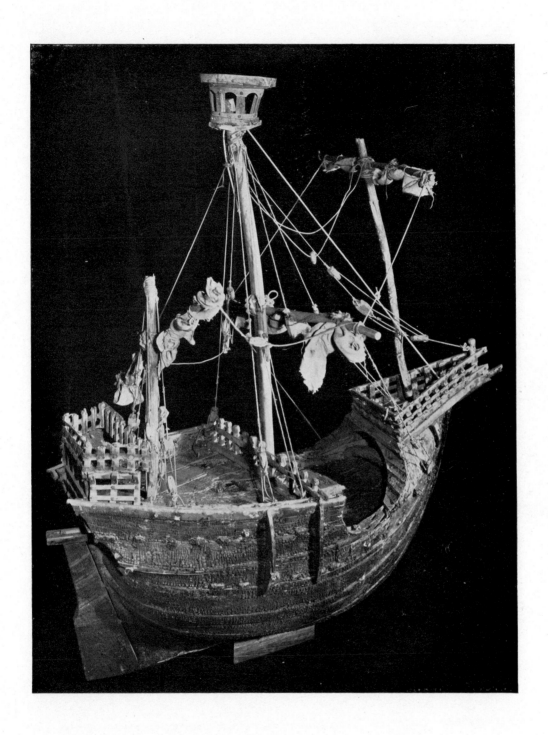

PLATE 1.
"CHURCH-SHIP," *circa* 1450. FROM MATARÓ, CATALONIA, SPAIN
(*"Prins Hendrik"* Maritime Museum, Rotterdam)

PLATE 2.
GOLD CUP, 1503. FOUNDED ON THE "KRAECK" OF "W.A."
(Germanic National Museum, Nuremberg)

PLATE 3.
DETAIL OF CARPACCIO'S "PROCESSION IN A CHURCH,"
SHOWING VOTIVE "CHURCH-SHIPS"
(*Academy of Fine Arts, Venice*)
INTERIOR OF THE GROOTE KERK, HAARLEM
WITH COMMEMORATIVE "CHURCH-SHIPS"

PLATE 5.

FLEMISH MODEL OF GALLEON. END OF XVITH CENTURY

(*Museo Naval, Madrid*)

PLATE 6.
FLEMISH MODEL OF GALLEON. END OF XVIth CENTURY
ANOTHER VIEW, SHOWING DECORATION DETAIL
(*Museo Naval, Madrid*)

PLATE 7.
MODEL OF UNKNOWN ORIGIN, BUT APPARENTLY
A "CHURCH-SHIP," *circa* 1525
(*In the collection of the late Sir William Van Horne*)

PLATE 8.
FRENCH GALLEON, XVITH CENTURY
HANGING MODEL BY R. MORTON NANCE
(*Made for R. W. Mackenzie, Esq., Earlshall, Fife*)

PLATE 9.
VENETIAN "CHURCH-SHIP." MIDDLE OF XVITH CENTURY
(Museo Storico Navale, Venice)

PLATE 10.

ELIZABETHAN SHIP, 1590-1600
MODEL BY R. MORTON NANCE
(Made for Colonel Gascoigne, Lotherton Hall, Yorks.)

PLATE 11.
"CHURCH-SHIP," LATE XVITH CENTURY. WITH MONOGRAM OF
CHRISTIAN IV OF DENMARK ON STERN
RE-RIGGED *circa* 1720
(*Trinity House, Leith, Scotland*)

PLATE 12.
"CHURCH-SHIP" WITH PAINTED SAILS, DATED 1603
(Germanic National Museum, Nuremberg)

PLATE 13.
"CHURCH-SHIP," *circa* 1620
(*Groote Kerk, Haarlem*)

PLATE 14.
THE "SOVERAIGNE OF THE SEAS," 1637
MODEL BY HENRY B. CULVER, NEW YORK

PLATE 16.
HUDSON'S "HALVE MAEN" (HALF MOON), 1609
MODEL BY G. C. E. CRONE, AMSTERDAM

PLATE 17.
HUDSON'S "HALVE MAEN" (HALF MOON), 1609
MODEL BY G. C. E. CRONE, AMSTERDAM

PLATE 18.
DUTCH MAN-OF-WAR, 76 GUNS, *circa* 1675-1680
(Destroyed in the Hohenzollern Museum, Berlin, during the war.
A half-size copy is in the National Maritime Museum, Greenwich)

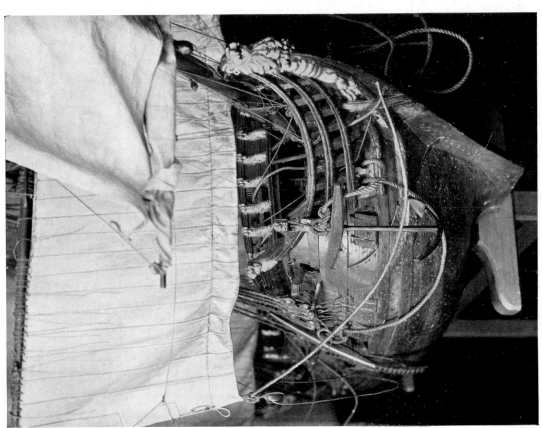

PLATE 20.

DUTCH MAN-OF-WAR, *circa* 1675-1680, BOW AND STERN
(Formerly in the Hohenzollern Museum, Berlin)

PLATE 21.
"CHURCH-SHIP," *circa* 1610
(*St. Mary's Church, Bergen*)

PLATE 22.

MODEL BELIEVED TO BE PHINEAS PETT'S "LITTLE SHIP," 1634

(Ashmolean Museum, Oxford)

PLATE 23.
THE "NORSKE LÖVE" (NORWEGIAN LION). BUILT AT LÜBECK, 1653
IVORY MODEL CARVED BY JAKOB JENSEN, 1654
(Rosenborg Castle, Copenhagen)

PLATE 24.
DUTCH FLIGHT, *circa* 1645
(*Nederlandsch Historisch Scheepvaart Museum, Amsterdam*

PLATE 25.
DUTCH EAST INDIAMAN, "PRINS WILLEM," 1651
(*Rijks Museum, Amsterdam*)

PLATE 26.
THE "AMARANTHE," 1654. REPLICA OF ORIGINAL MODEL IN
THE STATE COLLECTION, STOCKHOLM
(*Maritime Museum, Gothenburg*)

PLATE 27.
THE "ZEELANDIA," 1653. FLAGSHIP OF
ADMIRAL JAN EVERTSZEN, 1662
("*Prins Hendrik*" *Maritime Museum, Rotterdam*)

PLATE 28.
DUTCH MAN-OF-WAR, *circa* 1675. WITH RENOVATIONS OF LATER DATES
(Oudheidkundig Museum, Ghent)

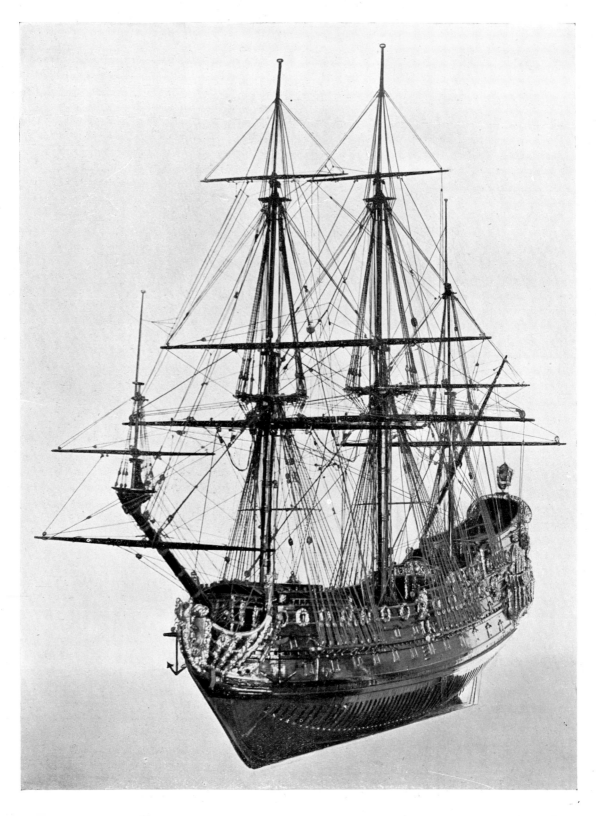

PLATE 29.
ENGLISH 90-GUN SHIP, *circa* 1675. PROBABLY AN EXPERIMENTAL MODEL
RIGGED BY MISS B. P. DERRICK AND DR. R. C. ANDERSON
(*National Maritime Museum, Greenwich*)

PLATE 30.
THE "PRINCE," FIRST-RATE LINE-OF-BATTLE SHIP
BUILT AT CHATHAM, 1670, BY PHINEAS PETT
(*Science Museum, South Kensington*)

PLATE 31.
DANISH THREE-DECKER, "CHRISTIANUS QUINTUS," 1673. MODERN MODEL
(*Danish Admiralty, Copenhagen*)

PLATE 32.
ENGLISH ROYAL YACHT, *circa* 1685
(*National Maritime Museum, Greenwich*)
THE "ROYAL JAMES," 100 GUNS, 1671
(*Royal United Services Museum, London*)

PLATE 33.
ENGLISH YACHT, *circa* 1690
(*In the possession of Dr. R. C. Anderson*)

BOW OF 100-GUN SHIP, *circa* 1670
(*National Maritime Museum, Greenwich*)

PLATE 34.
"LA RÉALE," FRENCH "ADMIRAL GALLEY," 1690–1715
(Musée de Marine, Paris)

PLATE 35.
DANISH TWO-DECKER "CHURCH-SHIP." LATE XVIITH CENTURY
WITH XIXTH-CENTURY RENOVATIONS
(*Kunstgewerbe Museum, Flensburg*)

PLATE 36.
DUTCH MAN-OF-WAR "HOLLANDIA," 82 GUNS, 1665-1683
(*Nederlandsch Historisch Scheepvaart Museum, Amsterdam*)

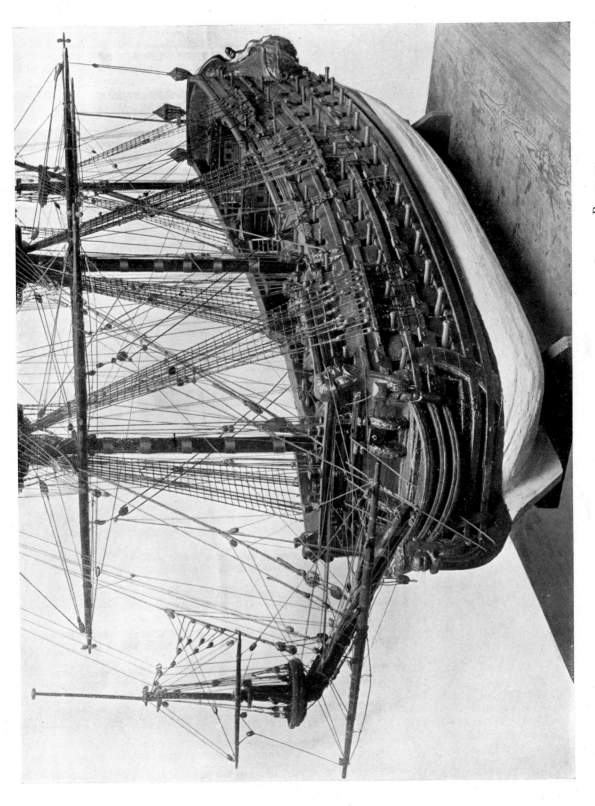

PLATE 37.

DUTCH 93-GUN SHIP, *circa* 1685. RIGGED BY DR. R. C. ANDERSON
AND PRESENTED BY HIM TO THE MUSEUM
(*Nederlandsch Historisch Scheepvaart Museum, Amsterdam*)

PLATE 38.
THE "CORONATION," 90 GUNS, 1686
RIGGED BY DR. R. C. ANDERSON AND L. A. PRITCHARD
(Formerly in the London Museum)

PLATE 39.
HANGING "CHURCH-SHIP" TYPE MODEL OF
A LÜBECK FLIGHT. DATED 1690 ON STERN,
BUT WITH XVIIITH-CENTURY JIB-BOOM
FROM A DRAWING BY R. MORTON NANCE
(Hall of the Schiffergesellschaft, Lübeck)

PLATE 40.
NORWEGIAN "CHURCH-SHIP." WITH LEGEND "DEN
FORGYLTE SVAN (THE GILDED SWAN), ANNO 1691"
ON STERN. RIGGING PARTLY CONTEMPORARY
(*Bergens Museum, Bergen*)

PLATE 41.
NORWEGIAN "CHURCH-SHIP." END OF XVIITH CENTURY
WITH ORIGINAL RIGGING
(*Bergens Museum, Bergen*)

PLATE 42.
GENOESE "CHURCH-SHIP." END OF XVIITH CENTURY
WITH ORIGINAL RIGGING
(Palazzo Bianco, Genoa)

PLATE 43.
FRENCH LINE-OF-BATTLE SHIP, "LE ROYAL-LOUIS," 1692
(*Musée de Marine, Paris*)

PLATE 44.
ENGLISH ADMIRALTY YACHT, "THE NAVY," 1672
(*From the Cuckfield Park Collection. Bequeathed by Colonel Rogers to the
United States Naval Academy Museum, Annapolis, Maryland*)

R. Morton Nance
1902

PLATE 45.
"L'Agréable," French Two-Decker, 1695
From a Drawing by R. Morton Nance
(*Musée de Marine, Paris*)

PLATE 46.
ENGLISH 80-GUN SHIP, 1695
(*From the Cuckfield Park Collection. Bequeathed by Colonel Rogers to the
United States Naval Academy Museum, Annapolis, Maryland*)

PLATE 47.
ENGLISH 50-GUN SHIP, DATED 1703
ENGLISH 80-GUN SHIP, *circa* 1695
*(From the Cuckfield Park Collection. Bequeathed by Colonel Rogers to the
United States Naval Academy Museum, Annapolis, Maryland)*

PLATE 48.
ENGLISH 50-GUN SHIP, 1695
(*From the Cuckfield Park Collection. Bequeathed by Colonel Rogers to the*
United States Naval Academy Museum, Annapolis, Maryland)

PLATE 49.

VENETIAN TRADING GALEASS, DATED 1726
(Musée de Marine, Paris)

ENGLISH 54-GUN SHIP, circa 1710
(From the Cuckfield Park Collection. Bequeathed by Colonel Rogers to the
United States Naval Academy Museum, Annapolis, Maryland)

PLATE 50.
GENOESE GALLEY. END OF XVIIth CENTURY
(*Palazzo Bianco, Genoa*)

PLATE 53.
THE "ST. GEORGE," SECOND-RATE, 96 GUNS, 1701
(From the Cuckfield Park Collection. Bequeathed by Colonel Rogers to the
United States Naval Academy Museum, Annapolis, Maryland)

PLATE 54.
DANISH FRIGATE OF THE TIME OF TORDENSKJOLD, 1691-1720
(Kronborg Museum, Elsinore)

PLATE 55.
THE "MARLBOROUGH," 90 GUNS. RIGGED BY DR. R. C. ANDERSON
(*Formerly in the London Museum*)

PLATE 56.
ENGLISH 50-GUN SHIP, 1690-1700
(National Maritime Museum, Greenwich)

PLATE 57.
DECKS OF THE "BRITANNIA," 1700
*(From the Cuckfield Park Collection. Bequeathed by Colonel Rogers to the
United States Naval Academy Museum, Annapolis, Maryland)*

PLATE 58.
DETAILS OF STERN AND BOW OF THE "BRITANNIA," 1700
*(From the Cuckfield Park Collection. Bequeathed by Colonel Rogers to the
United States Naval Academy Museum, Annapolis, Maryland)*

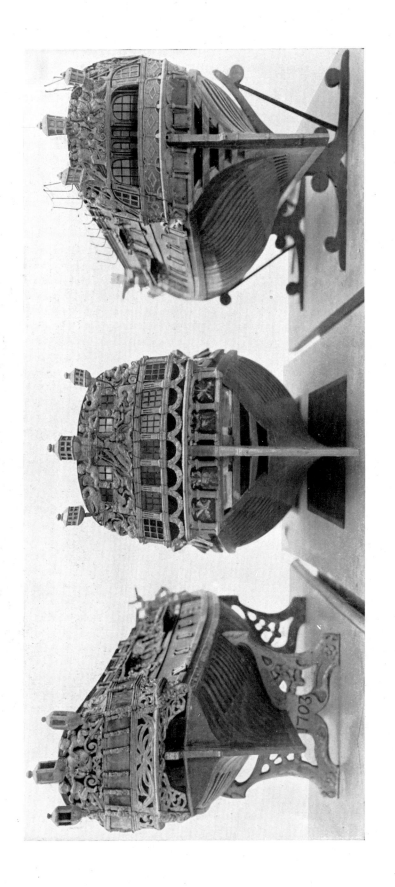

PLATE 59.

STERNS OF ENGLISH 50-GUN SHIP OF 1705; ENGLISH 60-GUN SHIP,
BEGINNING OF XVIIIth CENTURY; AND ENGLISH
54-GUN SHIP OF 1710

(From the Cuckfield Park Collection. Bequeathed by Colonel Rogers to the
United States Naval Academy Museum, Annapolis, Maryland)

PLATE 60.
ENGLISH 60-GUN SHIP. BEGINNING OF XVIIIth CENTURY
RESTORED AND RIGGED BY HENRY B. CULVER
(Bequeathed by Colonel Rogers to the United States
Naval Academy Museum, Annapolis, Maryland)

PLATE 61.
ENGLISH HOY, 1700-1730
MODEL BY R. MORTON NANCE
(*On exhibition at the Science Museum, South Kensington*)

PLATE 62.

SMALL ENGLISH VESSEL, PROBABLY A SNOW, *circa* 1705
(In the possession of Dr. R. C. Anderson)

ENGLISH SHIP OF 20-24 GUNS, *circa* 1705
(National Maritime Museum, Greenwich)

PLATE 63.

ENGLISH FOURTH-RATE MAN-OF-WAR, 60 GUNS
BUILT *circa* 1715, ON THE ESTABLISHMENT OF 1706
(Science Museum, South Kensington; lent by H. J. Dafforne, Esq.)

PLATE 64.

ENGLISH THIRD-RATE LINE-OF-BATTLE SHIP, 1719 ESTABLISHMENT
(Science Museum, South Kensington; lent by the Executors of Mrs. Humphry)

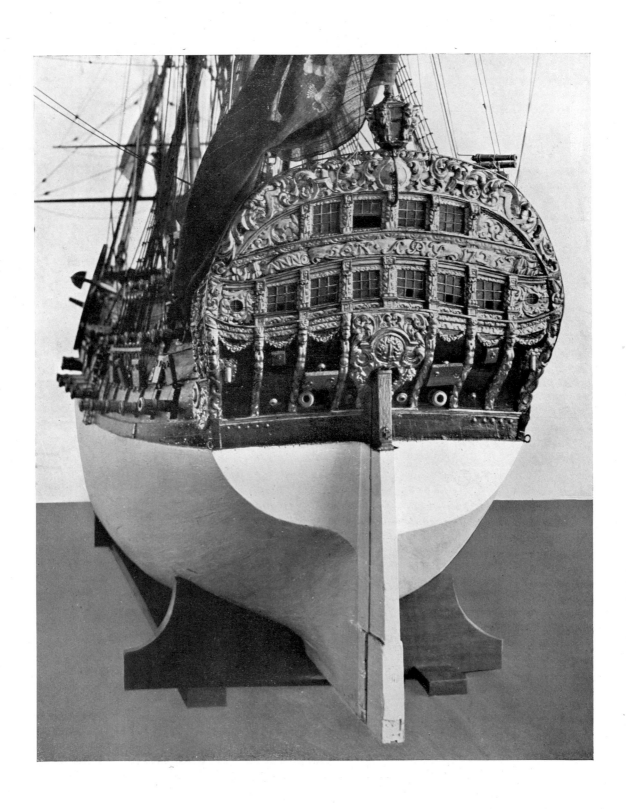

PLATE 65.
DUTCH EAST-INDIAMAN "DEN ARY," 54 GUNS, 1725
(*Nederlandsch Historisch Scheepvaart Museum, Amsterdam*)

PLATE 66.

60-GUN SHIP, POSSIBLY SPANISH, *circa* 1730
(*National Maritime Museum, Greenwich*)

ENGLISH 70-GUN SHIP, *circa* 1730-1735
(*In the possession of Dr. R. C. Anderson*)

PLATE 67.
THE "ROYAL WILLIAM," 100 GUNS
BUILT 1719. RIGGING MODERN
(*National Maritime Museum, Greenwich*)

PLATE 68.
THE "ROYAL WILLIAM," 100 GUNS. BUILT 1719
(Bequeathed by Colonel Rogers to the United States
Naval Academy Museum, Annapolis, Maryland)

PLATE 69.
ENGLISH SHIP, PROBABLY THE "ROYAL GEORGE," 1715
(Technische Hochschule, Hanover)

Photo. Max Baumann

PLATE 70.
STERN OF ENGLISH SHIP, PROBABLY THE "ROYAL GEORGE," 1715
(*Technische Hochschule, Hanover*)

PLATE 71.
ENGLISH THIRD-RATE LINE-OF-BATTLE SHIP
EARLY XVIIIth CENTURY
(Science Museum, South Kensington; lent by P. E. D. Hammond, Esq.)

PLATE 72.
SPANISH 34-GUN FRIGATE "LA FLORA," 1742
(*Museo Naval, Madrid*)

PLATE 73.

MALTESE GALLEY. FIRST HALF OF XVIIITH CENTURY
(National Maritime Museum, Greenwich; presented to the
Royal Naval Museum by the Duke of Northumberland, 1828)

PLATE 74.
DUTCH EAST-INDIAMAN, *circa* 1740
(*Rijks Museum, Amsterdam*)

PLATE 75.

THE "VICTORY," 100 GUNS. BUILT 1737. LOST, WITH
ADMIRAL SIR JOHN BALCHEN AND ALL HANDS, ON THE CASQUETS, 1744
(National Maritime Museum, Greenwich)

PLATE 76.

FRENCH LINE-OF-BATTLE SHIP "LE BIEN-AIMÉ." PERIOD OF LOUIS XV
(Musée de Marine, Paris)

PLATE 77.
DANISH 50-GUN SHIP "FYN," 1746
(*Danish Admiralty, Copenhagen*)

PLATE 78.
MODEL OF A DUTCH SHIP, *circa* 1740
FROM A DRAWING BY R. MORTON NANCE
(*Musée de Marine, Paris*)

PLATE 79.
DUTCH EAST-INDIAMAN "DE JONKVROUW CATHARINA CORNELIA"
MIDDLE OF XVIIITH CENTURY
(*"Prins Hendrik" Maritime Museum, Rotterdam*)

PLATE 80.

SPANISH TWO-DECKER. FIRST HALF OF XVIIITH CENTURY
SHOWN AS LAID UP FOR WINTER
(Museo Naval, Madrid)

PLATE 81.
DUTCH ADMIRALTY YACHT, *circa* 1750
(*Nederlandsch Historisch Scheepvaart Museum, Amsterdam*)

PLATE 82.

FRENCH LINE-OF-BATTLE SHIP "LE SANS-PAREIL," 108 GUNS, 1760
(Musée de Marine, Paris)

PLATE 83.
SWEDISH EAST-INDIAMAN, 1750
(*Maritime Museum, Gothenburg*)

PLATE 85.
FRENCH FRIGATE. PERIOD OF LOUIS XVI
(*Musée de Marine, Paris*)

PLATE 86.
DUTCH MERCHANTMAN "RUST EN WERK"
(REST AND WORK), 1780
("*Prins Hendrik*" *Maritime Museum, Rotterdam*)

PLATE 87.
ENGLISH FRIGATE, 24 GUNS. BUILT *circa* 1750
(Science Museum, South Kensington)

Plate 88.
English Sloop of War, Schooner-rigged, *circa* 1780
(Science Museum, South Kensington)

PLATE 90.
DUTCH FRIGATE "WAGENINGEN," *circa* 1780
(*Musée de Marine, Paris*)

PLATE 91.
PRIVATEER "NEPTUNUS." MODERN MODEL
FROM PLANS BY CHAPMAN
(*Maritime Museum, Gothenburg*)

PLATE 92.
SPANISH CHEBEC OF THE TYPE BUILT FOR ATTACKING
THE FORTIFICATIONS OF ALGIERS, 1783
(*Museo Naval, Madrid*)

PLATE 93.
FRENCH LINE-OF-BATTLE SHIP "L'ARTÉSIEN," 64 GUNS, 1774-1786
(Musée de Marine, Paris)

PLATE 94.
SPANISH 112-GUN SHIP "REAL CARLOS." BUILT AT HAVANA, 1787
(*Museo Naval, Madrid*)

PLATE 95.
SWEDISH ROYAL YACHT "AMPHION." BUILT BY CHAPMAN, 1779
(State Naval History Collections, Stockholm)

PLATE 96.
"DIE VERÄNDERUNG" (THE CHANGE). FLENSBURG
TRADING SNOW OF 1794. MODERN MODEL
(*Altonaer Museum, Altona*)

PLATE 98.
AMERICAN MERCHANTMAN "ARM AND HOPE"
BUILT PROVIDENCE, R.I., 1796
(*In the possession of Mr. Clarkson A. Collins jr., New York*)

PLATE 100.
DUTCH BOOTSCHIP "DE GOEDE HOOP" (GOOD HOPE)
END OF XVIIITH CENTURY
(*Nederlandsch Historisch Scheepvaart Museum, Amsterdam*)

PLATE 101.

SNOW "RISING STATES." LATE XVIIITH CENTURY
(Peabody Museum of Salem, Mass.)

PLATE 102.
PINKSHIP-RIGGED WEST-INDIAMAN "DORIS"
FLENSBURG, 1800. MODERN MODEL
(*Altonaer Museum, Altona*)

PLATE 103.

74-Gun Line-of-Battle Ship "Ajax," Built at Rotherhithe, 1795-1798
(Science Museum, South Kensington)

PLATE 104.
ENGLISH FRIGATE "AEOLUS," 1801. BONE PRISONER-OF-WAR MODEL
(Science Museum, South Kensington)

PLATE 105.
DUTCH LINE-OF-BATTLE SHIP "CHATTAM," 76 GUNS, 1800
(Rijks Museum, Amsterdam)

PLATE 106.

FRENCH LINE-OF-BATTLE SHIP "L'ACHILLE," 1803

(Musée de Marine, Paris)

PLATE 107.

THIRD-RATE LINE-OF-BATTLE SHIP "HERO," 74 GUNS
BUILT ON THE THAMES, 1803. RIGGING BY J. T. MAJOR, 1921
(Science Museum, South Kensington; lent by Sir Alan H. Moore, Bart.)

PLATE 108.
PRIVATEER "AMERICA," OF THE WAR OF 1812
BUILT AT SALEM
(*Peabody Museum of Salem, Mass.*)

PLATE 110.

FRENCH BOMB-KETCH, 8 GUNS AND 2 MORTARS, 1815

(*Musée de Marine, Paris*)

PLATE 111.
80-GUN TWO-DECKER "VANGUARD." BUILT AT PEMBROKE, 1835
(Science Museum, South Kensington)

PLATE 112.
BRIG-RIGGED SLOOP OF WAR "FANTÔME"
LAUNCHED AT CHATHAM, 1839
(Science Museum, South Kensington)

PLATE 113.
AMERICAN WHALER, *circa* 1850
(*Old Dartmouth Historical Society, New Bedford, Mass.*)

PLATE 114.

FRENCH 80-GUN SHIP "L'HERCULE," 1835

(In the possession of Mons. Jacques Sottas, Paris)

PLATE 115.

The "Java," Clipper-type Merchantman. Built at Hamburg, 1852

(Altonaer Museum, Altona)

PLATE 116.
REVENUE CUTTER, 14 GUNS, 1810-1830
(*Science Museum, South Kensington*)

PLATE 117.
THE "GREAT REPUBLIC," AMERICAN CLIPPER
BUILT AT BOSTON, MASS., 1853
(Musée de Marine, Paris)

PLATE 118.
THE "YOUNG AMERICA," BUILT AT NEW YORK, 1853, BY WILLIAM H. WEBB
(Formerly in the Carlton Chapman Collection)

PLATE 120.

THE "CALIFORNIA," LAST WHITE STAR SAILING CLIPPER. BUILT AT BELFAST, 1890

(Science Museum, South Kensington; lent by the Oceanic Steam
Navigation Company, Ltd.)

LIST OF THE PRINCIPAL MUSEUMS AND OTHER INSTITUTIONS IN EUROPE AND AMERICA CONTAINING SHIP MODELS

This list has been compiled by Frank G. G. Carr, Director of the National Maritime Museum, Greenwich, London, S.E.10., from the latest information obtained by direct contact with the Museums and countries concerned. The compiler wishes to record his thanks to more than fifty correspondents who have assisted in assembling these notes.

GREAT BRITAIN

LONDON. National Maritime Museum, Greenwich, S.E.10. Director: Frank G. G. Carr, M.A., LL.B. The Museum, covering with its grounds 11½ acres, and having nearly ¾-mile of galleries, is filled with a rich collection of maritime treasures, pictures, models, and relics of all kinds. Models include a representative series of Navy Board dockyard contemporary models of 17th and 18th Centuries; Admiralty block models and accurate scale models of the 19th and 20th Centuries; Royal yachts of the 17th and 18th Centuries, also steam yachts of the Victorian era; British and foreign merchant ships, from crude 18th-century barks to 19th-century clipper ships; a large series of builders' scale models of 20th-century merchant ships; a miscellaneous collection of Foreign men-of-war; constructional models of British ships of the 18th Century; hoys, cutters, troop landing boats, fireships etc., of the 18th and 19th Centuries, and fishing craft, barges etc. The Museum also possesses the complete series of Admiralty draughts of all types of ships built in the early 18th Century and down to 1837, numbering nearly 4,000; there is a small collection of merchant ship draughts of the 19th Century, and a series of plans of types of British coastal craft in the last days of sail. The library contains over 10,000 manuscripts, as well as a large collection of maritime books, ancient and modern, which can be studied in the Students' Room provided.

Science Museum (Ministry of Education), Exhibition Road, South Kensington, S.W.7. Director: Dr. H. Shaw, A.R.C.S. The Water Transport Collections contain an important series of contemporary models of sailing ships-of-war of the 17th, 18th and 19th Centuries, a number of them rigged, in addition to a representative group of models of steam and motor ships and miscellaneous small craft from all parts of the world. Official Handbooks:—"Sailing Ships", Part I (4s.), and Part II (3s. 6d.); "British Fishing-boats and Coastal Craft" (printing); "Merchant Steamers and Motor-ships" (printing).

Imperial War Museum, Lambeth Road, S.E.1. Director: L. R. Bradley, O.B.E. The Naval side of the Museum includes models of naval and merchant ships which took part in the wars of 1914-18 and 1939-45; many paintings and drawings illustrating the wars; and a collection of over a quarter of a million official photographs concerning every naval activity during the wars. There is an extensive library of books of maritime interest.

Royal United Service Museum, Whitehall, S.W.1. Secretary: Capt. E. Altham, C.B., R.N. Warship models have been a special feature of the collections for over 100 years. There are examples of fighting ships from the 16th Century to the very latest additions to His Majesty's Navy.

Trinity House, Tower Hill, E.C.3. The small but fine collection of ship models were mostly destroyed in the war; and, apart from models of lightships now exhibited in the National Maritime Museum and the Science Museum, there are at Tower Hill only the St. Goven light vessel (old type); Smith's Knoll light vessel (new type); and a bone model of H.M.S. *Foudroyant*.

BIDEFORD. Public Library and Museum. Curator: Miss M. E. Jenkinson. The collections include a few ship models of vessels built locally, or with local associations, old and modern; and range from the silver model of an Elizabethan ship to a model of H.M.S. *Bideford* (1942). A well-decked steamship; brig; barque; barquentine; ship; wooden tug; and gravel barge (1830), are exhibited; and there are various maritime pictures, trophies and relics.

BRISTOL. City Museum, Queen's Road. Director: F. S. Wallis, D.SC., PH.D. Included here are contemporary dockyard models of *Arethusa* (1781), *Mars* (1779), *Medea* (1778), and *Melampus* (1786). Stroud collection of model ships, beginning with a Roman galley and passing through successive stages to H.M.S. *Victory*. Other models include *Cutty Sark; Tom Cod* (the last Bristol Slave Ship); and examples made by the French prisoners-of-war.

CARDIFF. National Museum of Wales. Director: Dr. J. Dilwyn John. Models of sailing ships, principally of Welsh interest, and of cargo-carrying steamers in Welsh ownership showing development from 1870 to 1920. There are also paintings and photographs illustrating (a) the development of sailing ships and (b) shipbuilding on the Welsh coast.

CHANNEL ISLANDS. *See* GUERNSEY.

CHATHAM. Dockyard Museum. Open on application to the Admiral Superintendent. Directions from Police at Main Gate. Really fine collection of figure-heads around the Dockyard. Museum contains two original contemporary Commissioners' Barges; working models of dockyard gates; a sheer hulk, and other dockyard exhibits; full-size Indian birch-bark canoe; and a few small ship models, including one of a *Penelope* class cruiser.

DUNDEE. Public Libraries, Museums and Fine Art Galleries. Chief Librarian and Curator: J. Duncan Dundas, J.P. Collections contain models of Arctic Whalers *Narwhal* (1856) and *Hope* (1873); also early 19th-century warships *Caledonia, Prosperity, Lord Duncan,* and an unnamed 92-gun ship; mid-18th-century French *Foudroyant;* Spanish Galleon; Barques *Asia,* and *Marion Crosley;* Schooner *Ellengowan;* Paddle-steamer *Rose;* Oil Tanker *Dosina;* and 20 half models of named Screw Steamships.

EDINBURGH. Royal Scottish Museum. Director: Douglas A. Allan, D.SC., PH.D., F.R.S.G.S., F.R.S.E. The Technological department contains a representative collection of models of ships-of-war and merchantmen from Roman times to the present day. Reconstructions of such early Scottish warships as the *Yellow Carvel* (1480) and *Great Michael* (1511) are shown. Early English types include the hoy and brig. Many of the models are fully rigged and carry sails. Among contemporary models, outstanding examples are *D'Bataviase Eeuw,* a Dutch East Indiaman of 1719; a 120-gun ship of 1794; and a ship-rigged sloop (1825-1830). There is a series of French prisoner-of-war models. Special reference is due to the series of coastal and fishing craft, many of them ribbed and planked and carrying detailed equipment. A full range of Scottish types, many now extinct, is exhibited.

Naval and Military Museum, The Castle. Curator: Major H. P. E. Periera. Contains a few models, including the *Yellow Carvel* (1468); *Margaret* (1506); *Great Michael* (1511); and a dockyard model of H.M.S. *Ripon*. The collection also includes a number of uniforms etc., and other Scottish naval relics.

GLASGOW. Art Galleries and Museum. Director: Dr. T. J. Honeyman. The collection embraces models from the dug-out canoe of prehistoric times to the great modern liners and warships of the past decade. Recently there has been added the famous collection bequeathed by the late Colonel C. L. Spencer, D.S.O. These represent sailing vessels of the 18th and early 19th Centuries, and are mostly models made by French prisoners-of-war. The Napier model, Admiralty Dockyard production, of H.M.S. *Oxford* (1727) survived the air raid of 1941, and remains the most treasured of its class in the collection.

Steamship models range from the contemporary model of P.S. *Comet* to the passenger liner *Empress of Britain;* and warships from H.M. Troopship *Malabar* (1866) to the Battleship H.M.S. *Howe* (1942). Clyde pleasure steamers are well represented. Motor vessels include the 25,550 tons *Stirling Castle* and the 11,063 tons cargo vessel *Essex*.

GUERNSEY. Lukis and Island Museum, St. Barnabas, Cornet Street, St. Peter Port. Curator: J. M. V. Trotter. Contains naval and maritime relics which are connected with the history of the Island. Models of local craft include a Guernsey-built full-rigged ship; brig *James and Agnes;* 12-ton deep-sea fishing boat and small inshore fishing boat. Both these fishing craft are 3-masted, with a local rig developed from the French 3-masted lugger, and can spread a large area of canvas in light winds to stem the strong currents in local waters.

HASTINGS. Public Museum and Art Gallery, John's Place. Curator: J. Manwaring Baines, B.SC., F.R.S.A., F.Z.S. Models of Hastings fishing craft, including elliptical stern type, beam trawl; truncated stern, otter trawl; old-fashioned half-deck, flat stern; and punt. French prisoner-of-war man-of-war; clipper ship; Revenue cutter (early 19th Century); schooner; East Indiaman *Britannia*; Lord Brassey's yacht *Sunbeam*.

HULL. Museum of Fisheries and Shipping, Pickering Park. Director: J. B. Fay. Exhibits illustrating the evolution of the fishing and shipping industries from the old whaling and fishing smack days to modern whaling and trawling methods, and from the "dug-out" to the modern transatlantic liner. The collection is particularly strong in relics relating to the Hull whaling trade and fishing industry. There are in all over 150 excellent models.

The Hull Trinity House, Trinity House Lane. Receiver and Warden's Clerk: P. J. Walkington. The Rooms of the Corporation of the Hull Trinity House contain many and varied objects relating to maritime subjects of interest. There is a valuable collection of paintings and pictures, many curios, and a collection of ship models. Among them are models of men-of-war; a contemporary model of a yacht of Queen Anne's; a model of the *Golden Hind*; and several illustrating various types of sailing vessels as well as models of modern steam vessels.

ILFRACOMBE. The Museum. Curator: Mervyn G. Palmer, F.R.G.S., M.B.O.U. Models include H.M.S. *Hood;* Cunard S.S. *Mauritania;* a 10-gun brig; the *Lynelda* hospital ship; full-rigged ship *Mary Ann;* sailing vessel *Elizabeth* of Ilfracombe; a double-topsail schooner; and a case containing 37 minute models, exquisitely made, of British and foreign warships (Italian, German, Spanish, Japanese, and United States).

LANCASTER. Public Library, Market Square. City Librarian and Curator: G. M. Bland, F.S.A., F.R.S.A., M.R.S.L. Ship models include *Thetis*, 93 feet on the gun deck, built at Lancaster, engaged against French at Dominica, 1804 (presented by her Captain); contemporary model of 64-gun line-of-battle ship (c. 1750); Lancaster built iron clipper ship *Wennington* (1865); Antwerp river boat; fast packet boat *Waterwitch No. 2*, in service between Lancaster and Kendal (1842); Belgian fishing lugger (1916).

LEITH. Trinity House of Leith, Kirkgate. Master: Capt. C. F. Mackellar. Models include *Royal Oak*, 64 guns (c. 1753); ship *Melbourne* of Leith; barque *Marion Crosbie*, 902 tons (1889); 4-masted barque *Alcides*, 2075 tons (1893); ship *Zuleika*, 1144 tons (1875); *Royal George*, 74-gun ship, contemporary model made for Admiral Rodney (1792); *La Belle Esperance*, the ship in which Mary of Lorraine sailed from France to Scotland.

LEWES. Anne of Cleves House, Southover. Assistant Curator: Petronelle Crouch. French prisoner-of-war model of a frigate; model of cross-channel paddle steamer *Excelsior*, driven by clockwork, and made by a shipwright living in Lewes, 1820-1875.

LIVERPOOL. Public Museums, Carnatic Hall, Elmswood Road. Acting Director: F. Lambert, C.B.E., M.A. Contains an extensive collection of sailing, steamship and other models to illustrate the development of the primitive craft into the modern motor vessel. Embodied in the main collection are sections showing various types of craft used in different branches of commerce (cable-layers, oil-tankers, trawlers, etc.); peculiarities of hull form, such as whaleback, corrugated and turret-decked ships, and a model of the first arc-form ship; also ships associated with the port of Liverpool (ferryboats, pilot boats, tugs, barges, and pleasure steamers). There are 17th- 18th- and 19th-century contemporary warship models; 40 French prisoner-of-war models; a large collection of British and Dutch sailing fishing craft; various native boats; and oil paintings of shipping.

MAIDSTONE. Museum and Art Gallery. Curator: L. R. A. Grove. Admiralty dockyard model, contemporary, of early 18th-century 70-gun ship; Sir Cloudesley Shovell's *James* galley (1681-1687); early 19th-century corvette *Charybdis*, fully rigged; cutter yacht *Eliza*. There are also various other exhibits of maritime interest, including relics.

MIDDLESBOROUGH. Dorman Memorial Museum. Curator: W. Lillie, A.L.A., F.R.S.A. A section on the first floor is devoted chiefly to ship models. About 50 in all, they consist largely of various types of sailing vessel, from a yawl to a full-rigged ship. Also included are models of South Sea Island canoes; catamarans; Venetian galley; Elizabethan warships; modern steamship; and a patrol boat. There is also an actual specimen of a prehistoric dug-out canoe; many photographs and pictures of local and other ships; and various relics of maritime interest.

NEWCASTLE-UPON-TYNE. Municipal Museum of Science and Industry, Exhibition Park, Great North Road. Executive Officer: Percy Parr. The Shipping Section contains examples of a very large number of ships of almost every type: early sailing men-of-war; clipper ships; early steam vessels; battleships; cruisers; destroyers; submarines; yachts; fishing vessels; cobles; lifeboats; a lightship; and a model of H.M.S. *Victoria* on the launching slip. There are also prints, drawings and photographs of all kinds of ships; and relics of the famous *Mauretania*. The museum also contains the actual bow, boiler and wheelhouse of the first turbine vessel *Turbinia*, with other early turbine relics.

NORWICH. Bridewell Museum of Local Industries. Curator: Miss G. V. Barnard. The collections include models of craft built or used locally; being craft on rivers and broads for trading or pleasure purposes, such as the extinct keel, the wherry, and the Norfolk yachts; fishing vessels, lifeboats etc., of Yarmouth and Lowestoft; and a maritime section of models of vessels bringing cargoes to local ports.

ORKNEY. *See* Stromness.

PETERBOROUGH. The Museum, Priestgate. Curator: M. Urwick Smith, B.A. The collections include several models in bone, fully rigged, of men-of-war, made by French prisoners-of-war at Norman Cross, near Peterborough, between the years 1796 and 1814; also a large model of a prisoner-of-war hulk.

PETERHEAD. Public Library and Arbuthnot Museum, St. Peter Street. Curator: Mrs. J. Knox. Collection includes 3 full-rigged ships, *Trafalgar; Poseidon;* and one unknown; 3-mast schooner *Rosebud;* full-rigged steam whalers *Eclipse* and *Hope;* and one frigate.

PLYMOUTH. City Museum and Art Gallery, Tavistock Road. Curator: A. A. Cumming. In view of Plymouth's intimate association with the history and development of shipping, the Museum contains an important collection of ship models illustrating the development from wood to steel and from sail to steam in the Royal and Merchant Navies. Of particular local interest is the model of the *Golden Hind* commemorating the circumnavigation of the world by Sir Francis Drake.

PORTSMOUTH. "Victory" Museum, H.M. Dockyard, Portsmouth. Curator: Commanding Officer, H.M.S. Victory. Under the general supervision of the Trustees of the National Maritime Museum, Greenwich. Contains relics of H.M.S. *Victory;* the state barge, built for Charles II, in which the body of Lord Nelson was conveyed from Greenwich to Whitehall Stairs; figure-heads of famous ships that ended their days at Portsmouth; relics of Lord Nelson, his officers and men; ship models of warships; paintings; miscellaneous items from H.M. Ships; and personal relics. A Panorama of Trafalgar, designed and painted by W. L. Wyllie, R.A., is viewed through a full-size reproduction of the stern windows of the French *Neptune*.

ROCHESTER. Eastgate House Museum. Hon. Curator: J. Herbert Bolton, F.Z.S. Collection includes French prisoner-of-war models of 100-gun ship (1800); 74-gun ship (1790); three 32-gun frigates; two barques, built 1881; stumpy barge; two model bawley boats; hoy *Spartan* (1804); and a barque, built 1830.

SHOREHAM. Marlipins Museum, High Street, Shoreham-by-Sea. Hon. Curator: Henry Cheal. Collections include frigate *Seringapatam*, 26 guns, East Indiaman, built Blackwall, 1837; 3-mast schooner *Crocodile;* two Shoreham-built vessels, the barque *Akbar*, and the brig *Charles*.

SOUTHAMPTON. Tudor House Museum, Bugle Street. Curator: Norman Cook, B.A. Collection includes bone model of H.M.S. *Temeraire*, with original rigging; contemporary model of Union Line *Moor* and *Trojan;* several reconstructions, including Southampton fishing hoy, early 19th Century. Also a series of 600 drawings of ships using Southampton Docks during the past 50 years, by A. E. Cozens.

SOUTH SHIELDS. Public Libraries, Museum and Art Room, Ocean Road. Borough Librarian: Harrison Burgess. Collection includes Wm. Wouldhave's original model from which the first lifeboat was built in 1789; other lifeboat models; pilot coble *Tyne* (1898); French prisoner-of-war model of French 52-gun ship *L'Amatone;* 3-masted government transport (1846); working model of early Tyne steam tug-boat (1863), being a most interesting contemporary model, capable of sailing under her own steam; various other models of different types of sailing and steamships; model of Noah's Ark, awarded third prize at Shipwright's Exhibition, 1947.

STROMNESS. Orkney Natural History Society Museum, 52 Alfred Street. Hon. Secretary: W. Towers. Collection of models of local interest, including London-Leith smack (1800-1840); brig *Golden Ace;* Geordie brig; schooners; wooden and iron sailing ships and steamships, including early paddle-wheel vessels; and local types of craft, among them the North Isles yole and the Flotta dinghy; there are also yacht models; a French prisoner-of-war warship; and the liner *Abosso*.

SUNDERLAND. Public Museum. Director: James Crawley. Contains models of Sunderland-built ships, comprising some 12 sailing ships, 15 steam ships and naval vessels; models of small craft, fishing cobles, etc.; a dug-out canoe dredged from the River Wear; a few models of marine engines; a small selection of ships' instruments; paintings and many prints and photographs of Sunderland-built ships and local shipyards.

SWANSEA. Royal Institution of South Wales. Hon. Secretary: W. H. Hanna. Small collection of ship models, from full-rigged ships to merchant steamers; pictures; collection of pictures of wrecks, which is privately owned, but may be seen by arrangement.

WEST HARTLEPOOL. Public Libraries, Gray Art Gallery and Museum. Director: R. Edgar Lyde, A.L.A. Collection includes models of brigantine *Mirage* (1854), first ship built at West Hartlepool; *British Queen*, sail and steam model; *Bellerophon*, 12-gun frigate; and the locally built steamships *Nunima; Marmion; Stawley* and *Digby*.

WHITBY. Whitby Museum, Pannett Park. Hon. Keeper: H. B. Browne, M.A. The collection of ship models numbers some 160 exhibits, from three inches to seven feet in length, and divided into three classes. Precise models for shipyard use include the steamships *Whitehall; Beemah; Normanby; Larpool; Bagdale;* and *Arndale*. Scale models with artistic value include the *Golden Hind;* H.M.S. *Endeavour;* H.M.S. *Resolution;* the clipper ship *Cutty Sark;* emigrant ship *Columbus* (1832); and *Monkshaven,* the last Whitby-built sailing ship. Prisoner-of-war bone models include ships of 50, 64, 74, and 100 guns. There is also a collection of small craft models, including a Scarborough trawler; Whitby collier brig; Newfoundland trader topsail schooner; lifeboats; cobles; and mules.

WORTHING. Museum and Art Gallery. Curator: Ethel Gerard, A.L.A. The Hargood Room contains naval relics of the Hargood family, including Nelson items, Trafalgar exhibits, and local lifeboat records. There are about a dozen ship models of different types all made by the late A. C. Jackson, of Worthing; and four other ship models.

BELGIUM

ANTWERP. *Musée de Marine.* Curator: Am. Dermul. Contains a fine collection of ship models, including contemporary models of the Belgian East Indiaman *Barbersteyn;* Dutch frigate of the late 18th Century; 2-decker *Caesar* of 1806-7; ¼-size model of state barge of Napoleon, 1810; early 19th-century galiot; Belgian brig-of-war *Duc de Brabant;* mid-19th-century barquentine; and many local types, including paviljoenpoon, garnaalknots, schokker, steenschuit, mosselhengst, pilot schooner, and modern steamship models. Also pictures, prints and drawings, and photographs. There is a good library, and a handbook is published.

DENMARK

COPENHAGEN. *Danish Admiralty Collection,* Naval Museum, Royal Dockyard. Director: The Dockyard Superintendent, Holmen, Copenhagen K. Fine contemporary models, fully rigged, of Danish ships-of-war, from the time of Frederich IV (1699-1730) to the 19th Century.

Rosenborg Castle, Rosenborg, Copenhagen K. Director: Count Trampe. Contains the Chronological Collection of the Kings of Denmark (Christian IV to Christian IX); three ivory models by J. J. Nordmand (17th Century); a prisoner-of-war model of a warship; and a model of a Royal Yacht.

ELSINORE. *Handels og Sjofartsmuseet* (Museum for Commerce and Shipping), Kronborg Castle. Director: Mr. K. H. Klem. Opened in 1915, it occupies 30 rooms and gives a picture of Commerce and Shipping (mostly Merchant) in Denmark, past and present. In addition to an elaborate collection of contemporary and modern pictures and models of ships, it has important sections dealing with nautical instruments and charts; the lifeboat service; lighthouse and buoyage service; shipbuilding, etc; and there is a library of books and manuscripts. An illustrated journal is published annually, and a series of "Publications on Maritime History" appears at intervals.

While the above Museum may be regarded as a Central Museum for Commerce and Shipping covering the whole of Denmark, there are several local Museums, for instance at Aabenraa and Dragor, with extensive maritime sections; while many provincial Museums have exhibits descriptive of the particular Province's ancient shipping.

FRANCE

PARIS. *Musée de Marine,* Palais de Chaillot (in the Louvre before World War II). Covers all that is related to naval or merchant shipping. Wood carvings of the *Grande Réale,* the flagship of Louis XIV's galleys, by Puget. Shows Napoleon's state barge high and dry. Paintings include J. Vernet's 16 views of French ports (1755-1765). The Louvre collection of ship models, by far the most important in the world, includes a few contemporary 18th-century models and has long been famous for two outstanding features: a practically exhaustive series of naval types existing at the last stage of the sailing man-of-war era, and

72

a similar one of exotic craft about the same time; but only a few samples of each are displayed in the new installation.

Conservatoire des Arts et Métiers. These collections, somewhat on the lines of the Science Museum, London, include a few models of ships or marine contraptions, old or modern.

Invalides. The *Musée de l'Armée* includes a few rooms devoted to the naval side of World War I.

BORDEAUX. *Musée Carrère*, in the Le Tondre suburb. This Museum of old weapons includes a collection of 33 ship models from the collection of Evrard, a friend and famulus of Admiral Paris, the renovator of the Louvre Marine Museum. Several first-class 18th-century models, with a few anachronic touches. The Museum, closed in 1929, has not yet been re-opened; and all the models have suffered from considerable neglect since 1925. Some repair work has been undertaken during 1947, and ten of the smaller models have been restored. The municipality is considering the creation of a Maritime Museum in the centre of the city.

BREST. *Arsenal.* The Museum in the naval dockyard includes a few models of men-of-war, from the 18th Century to modern times. Also souvenirs, etc. (including the sword which beheaded a British spy during the 18th-century wars). Most of the collection, which had been stored inland, has been preserved, and is about to be rearranged in Brest. Several beautiful old-type models which stood in Admiralty offices have been destroyed.

CHERBOURG. *Arsenal.* The naval dockyard Museum, which harboured a score or so of ship models, a few of which were of interest although long-neglected and fallen into decay, has been practically destroyed during the War. All this may also be said to apply to the dockyard Museum at Lorient.

DUNKIRK. The *Musée Municipal* includes a few marine articles; and interesting 18th-century pictures regarding the Franco-British differences about Dunkirk.

The *Musée Maritime*, belonging to the Chamber of Commerce, contains modern reconstruction models of 17th-century men-of-war, which are rather failures; but there is a fine collection of valuable models of local and North Sea fishing boats and traders.

LORIENT. See above under Cherbourg.

MARSEILLES. *Musée Maritime et Colonial*, Palais de la Bourse. Models from the *Ville-de-Marseille*, 74, of 1812 (7 ft. long) to the P. and O. *Mongolia*. Pictures, numerous engravings, medals, etc. Chief items covered: local history, Mediterranean shipping, Near East trades, 17th-century galleys.

NANTES. *Musée de Salorges.* In the birth-place of the French tinned food industry. An attractive small Museum of local marine developments. Models, contemporary pictures, etc., chiefly of local enterprise, including the Slave Trade. Has escaped destruction.

ROCHEFORT. *Musée Dick Lemoine* (Hôtel de Cheusses). Includes the old naval dockyard collections of ship models, from 18th-century men-of-war to early ironclads, and one large working model, fully rigged. Many of the models are conspicuous for anachronic restorations. Contains also instruments, ancient charts, souvenirs, etc. A Franco-Canadian section is in preparation.

SAINT MALO. A Museum of relics etc. of the famous privateers' era had been put together during the pre-War years in Duguay-Trouin's home, but has been completely destroyed during the War.

TOULON. The naval dockyard's collection of ship models, old and modern, is on permanent loan at the city's *Musée Municipal*. Several valuable models used to adorn Admiralty offices have been destroyed, as well as the double row of old figure-heads at the Prefecture Maritime.

ALGIERS. A Marine Museum has been in the making under the untiring efforts of Captain P. J. Bruhier. The first rooms, illustrating local shipping developments from Roman times to the Barbaresque era, have been inaugurated in 1948.

GERMANY

BERLIN. *Institut für Meereskunde an der Universität Berlin*. This is in the Russian Sector of Berlin and unfortunately no information about it is available at present. An unconfirmed report suggests that this Museum was completely destroyed, and surviving models were thrown out by the Russians, or presented as toys to the children.

Museum Schloss Monbijou (formerly *Hohenzollern Museum*). This building and its contents were completely destroyed in the war.

ALTONA. *Altonaer Museum*. Director: Dr. Hubert Stierling. Most of the building was destroyed but, in the part still standing at the back, exhibitions are held of selections from the collection of models which survived the war intact, and which includes about 30 whole models and 40 half models of ocean and coastal trading vessels of various kinds—frigates; snows; schooners; brigs; etc., built in the Schleswig-Holstein shipyards in the 19th Century. Particularly rich in small coasters—Bojer; Eiderschnigge; Ever (Elb-, Lägerdorfer-, Ostsee-, Rhin-, and Galleasse-Ever); Galleasse; Galiot; Jacht; Kuff; Lühejolle; and Störprahm. There is an important Fishery Section, including whaling; and one original primitive boat, carved out of a single tree, from Ellerbeck, near Kiel. The models are supplemented by general maritime exhibits and a good collection of pictures and plans.

BREMEN. *Rathaushalle*(Town Hall). This survived the war, and contains various hanging models of old ships. No maritime museum is open at present, as the models and other objects are stored away until suitable premises become available.

Kolonia-und-Übersee Museum. Had a large collection of models and actual primitive sailing craft; destroyed.

Focke-Museum. This contained a collection of old models; completely destroyed.

EMDEN, OSTFRIESLAND. *Rathaus Sammlung* (Town Hall). Completely destroyed. One model, of an East Indiaman armed as a man-of-war of 60 guns, is at present stored in a bunker in Emden. There are no models of the church-ship type.

FLENSBURG, SCHLESWIG-HOLSTEIN. *Städtisches Museum*. Director: Dr. Fuglsang. Complete and open. Collections include original models of ships, one being of the Danish warship *Urania* (1690); pictures of ships of the Flensburg merchant fleet; sextants, octants, Jacob's staff, compasses, etc.; and implements, harpoons and knives for whaling.

HAMBURG. *Museum für Hamburgische Geschichte*. Director: Prof. Dr. Walter Hävernik. The Museum has a Department devoted to Hamburg navigation, and is again open. There are about 80 ship models (some of which have been badly damaged in the war), which include about 25 of older types of the 18th and 19th Centuries; 10 models, late 19th Century; and steamship models of different types. The collections also contain about 200 photographs and paintings of Hamburg ships.

HANOVER. *Technische Hochschule*. The most important model, fully rigged, is of an English man-of-war. The name of the ship is disputed. It was originally stated to be the *Royal George* of 1715; but Captain Walter Brandt of Detmold, Schanze, who restored the model in 1942-3, asserts that it is undoubtedly the *Victory IV* of 1737-44.

LÜBECK. *Museum für Kunst und Kulturgeschichte St. Annen*. Director: Dr. Gräbke. This Museum with its models survived intact, and is open to the public occasionally. Contains a small collection of old models, some rather rough, including *Die Hoffnung von Lübeck* and *Der Lowe;* scientifically reconstructed models of Hanseatic ships *der Adler* and *Jesus von Lübeck;* and documents, logs and other objects relating to the history of the Hansa.

74

MUNICH. *Deutsches Museum von Meisterwerken der Naturwissenschaft und Technik, Museum-sinsel.* Before the war there was a collection of about 50 models representing various types of ships from 3500-3000 B.C. to the oil tankers and motor cargo ships of to-day; in which the sailing-ship models included one of the *Great Harry;* a 20th-century 5-master; and the Antarctic ship *Gauss.* The maritime section was completely destroyed in an air raid on 12th July, 1944. At present there is no intention of rebuilding the Section owing to technical difficulties and lack of funds. Some parts of the collection are still in existence but are badly damaged; they are packed in depots.

NÜREMBERG. *Germanisches Nazionalmuseum.* Director: Dr. Günther Troche. The museum building was badly damaged in the war; parts of it have been rebuilt and some galleries are open to the public, but the maritime collections are stored, undamaged, in various depots. They contain models of warships, merchant vessels and small craft of various dates from the 16th Century; among them an armed merchant ship with the arms of the Pellers, of Nüremberg, 1603.

SCHLESWIG-HOLSTEIN. In addition to the Museums at Altona, Flensburg, and Lübeck, the following Provincial Museums contain maritime exhibits:—

Heimatmuseum Burg a. Fehmarn. Director: Bauer Wiepert. A model of a ship and pictures of sailing ships of Fehmarn shipping.

Museum Dithmarscher Vorgeschichte, Heide. Director: Dr. Kamphausen. Log canoe of the iron age; models of prehistoric boats up to Viking ship.

Heimatmuseum, Helgoland. The collection, dealing with pilotage, navigation instruments, and models of boats, was destroyed in the war.

Ludwig Nissen-Museum, Husum. Director: Dr. Wuhlenberg. Model of a Hanse ship (cog); foghorn, and a wooden ring for the fore sail of Langeness; mud sledge for fishing and hunting on the Watt of Langeness; figure-head; and octant.

Gedächtnishalle, Idstedt. Contains objects relating to the destruction of the Danish ship of line *Christian VIII,* off Eckernförde in 1848. Collection stored at present.

Friesenmuseum, Keitum, Sylt. Director: Kap. Jansen. Nautical instruments for measuring the altitude from Jacob's staff to octant; ship models of the 19th Century; figure-head, sea chest, charts, and pictures of ships of the 18th and 19th Centuries; log canoe (dug-out).

Brandschutzmuseum, Kiel. Director: Herr Kock. Models of steamships with lighting, fixtures, and fire extinguishing apparatus.

Volkerkunde Museum, Kiel. Director: Prof. Heise. Contains shipping section.

Heimatmuseum, Lauenburg. Director: Herr Götze. Original models of Elbe boats and Stecknitz boats of the 18th Century; representative utensils of the Lauenburg shipmaster's guild; documents relating to Elbe shipping dating from 1417.

Heimatmuseum, Mölln. Director: L. Peters. Models of ships; sextant.

Kreismuseum, Neustadt. Dug-out of the iron age; ship models and name board; pictures of the sea battle of von der Tann off Neustadt.

Museum vorgeschichtlicher Altertümer, Schleswig (Schloss Gottorp). Director: Dr. Kersten. Contains the important large Nydam boat; dug-outs; representations of boats on implements of the bronze age.

Heimatmuseum, Tönning. Director: Herr Hosch. Old ship models; 50 name boards of wrecked ships; life-belts; water barrels; figure-heads; bronze signal gun of 1759.

Seefahrermuseum, Westerland, Sylt. Director: Herr von Schilling. The collections, which are at present in store, contain objects of the Greenland Commandant Lorenz Petersen de Hahn, about 1700; reproduction of the cabin of his Greenland ship *Salomons Gericht;* whaling implements in great number; models and pictures from the sailing ship to the Hapag steamer; paintings of ships; implements for Watt navigation and ice boat sailing; nautical instruments; ships' lamps; signal and national flags; life saving apparatus of various kinds; name boards of wrecked ships; specimens of sailors' handiwork.

Friesenmuseum, Wyk auf Föhr. Director: Dr. Häberlein. Largely connected with the whaling industry from 1800 to 1870. Contains original models of ships; parts of ships; anchors and figure-heads; nautical instruments and books; log books; life saving apparatus; whaling implements and trophies; cabin of a whaler; objects from Greenland brought home by Föhr sailors.

HOLLAND

AMSTERDAM. *Nederlandsch Historisch Scheepvaart Museum*, Cornelis Schuystraat 57. The Museum contains a large number of models of men-of-war, merchantmen, fishing vessels, and inland water craft; also paintings, prints and drawings, navigational instruments, and an extensive maritime library.

Rijksmuseum. The historical section contains important paintings and a few models. The print room has many historical prints and drawings.

GRONINGEN. *Noordelijk Scheepvaartmuseum.* A number of models of merchantmen, coasters, etc., dating from the 19th and 20th Centuries; especially ships in use on the Northern coasts of the Netherlands.

HAARLEM. *Groote Kerk of St. Bavo.* Hanging models of ships.

ROTTERDAM. *Maritiem Museum "Prins Hendrik"*, Burg. s'Jacobplein 8. The Museum contains a large number of fishing vessels and inland water craft of all periods; also some paintings, prints and drawings, navigational instruments, globes and maps, and a collection of about 2,000 ships' draughts.

Instituut voor Scheepvaart en Luchtvaart, Rochussenstraat. The Institute has an extensive library and reference room dealing with shipping, navigation, machinery and aeronautics; and a Museum which contains models and machinery relating to these subjects.

SNEEK. *Friesch Scheepvaartmuseum.* Models of fishing vessels and inland watercraft.

ITALY

ROME. *Naval Historical Museum.* This is projected only, and it has not yet been decided where it is to be. It will comprise historical relics from the Italian Risorgimento (1821) up to the present day.

GENOA. *Civic Naval Museum.* Curator: Professor Carla Mazzarello. Collection contains models of Italian craft, as well as pictures, prints and drawings. Catalogue in preparation.

LA SPEZIA. *Naval Technical Museum.* Destroyed during the war, but has available material in process of re-organisation; owned by Ministry of Defence (Navy).

MILAN. *Naval Historical Museum*, situated in the Castello Sforzesco. Models, statues and relics of the navies of the Maritime Republics and of the Kingdom of Italy from 1870 onwards; owned by the Ministry of Defence (Navy).

VENICE. *Naval Historical Museum.* Director: Baron G. B. Rubin de Cervin. The collection consists of models, pictures, statues and relics up to the period of the Italian Risorgimento (1821); owned by Ministry of Defence (Navy).

MALTA

MALTA. *The Valletta Museum.* Contains a number of models, including a section of the warship *St. Joachim*, of the Order of St. John; frigate *La Vittoria*, of the last days of that Order; Maltese galley; Grand Master's barge and galley; the *Bucentaure;* Goze boats; and dghajsas. Also the silver mace of the Admiralty Court in Malta (abolished 1892).

76

NORWAY

OSLO. *Norsk Sjöfartsmuseum* (The Norwegian Maritime Museum), Bygdöy. Director: Kristian Kielland. Contains models of rowing, sailing and power-driven boats and ships, and a collection of original fishing boats from all parts of Norway, as well as figure-heads, boat equipment, and many pictures and drawings of vessels of all types. There are also sections on polar expeditions; whaling; fishing; light-house systems; and life-saving, etc.

Vikingskipshuset (The Viking Ship House), Bygdöy, Oslo. Director: Prof. A. W. Brögger. Contains three Viking ships found in Norway: the Oseberg, Gokstad, and Tune ships. There is also the equipment found in the Oseberg ship.

Framhuset (The *Fram* House), Bygdöy, Oslo. Chairman of *Fram* Committee: Eilif Ringnes. Contains the polar ship *Fram*, with her equipment. The *Fram* was used by Fridtjof Nansen on his polar expedition in 1893-1896: by Otto Sverdrup when he explored the regions north of America in 1898-1902; and by Roald Amundsen on his expedition to the South Pole in 1910-1912.

Norsk Folkemuseum (The Norwegian Folk Museum), Bygdöy, Oslo. Director: Reidar Kjellberg. Collection of models of the church-ship (votive) type.

BERGEN. *Bergens Sjöfartsmuseum* (Bergen Maritime Museum). Contains models of fishing boats and merchant vessels, together with figure-heads, boats' equipment, and pictures and drawings of boats and vessels of various Norwegian types.

Bergens Museum. Director: Prof. Björn Trompy. Models of church-ship (votive) type.

Museum of Fisheries. Considerable collections connected with fishing craft and methods.

HORTEN. *Marinemuseet* (The Norwegian Naval Museum), Carljohansvern, Horten. Curator: T. K. Olafsen. Contains several models of ships and equipment belonging to the Norwegian Navy; together with drawings of old warships, etc.

SANDEFJORD. *The Whaling Museum.* Contains the greatest collection in Norway dealing with the whaling industry.

STAVANGER. *Stavanger Sjöfartsmuseum* is part of Stavanger Museum and has collections of the same sort as those at Trondheim and Bergen.

TRONDHEIM. *Trondheims Sjöfartsmuseum* (Trondheim Maritime Museum). Curator: P. A. Gaustad. The collections, which are similar to those in the Bergen Maritime Museum, but of smaller extent, are exhibited in new rooms in the *Videnskapsselskapets Museum*, Museumsplass. There is also at Trondheim a Museum of Fisheries; but this is not open at present.

PORTUGAL

LISBON. *Museu de Marinha* (Maritime Museum). Temporarily situated in the *Escola Naval* (Naval College), Alfeite, Lisbon. Director: Commandante Jaime Correia do Inso. Originally consisted mainly of a valuable collection of 17th- and 18th-century models, from Royal Palaces, which the Sovereigns had presented to start the Museum. A fire in 1916 consumed the greater part of these models. The Museum's present day collection is made up of some models of galleys, galleons, caravels (lateen and rounded) of the time of the explorers; some saved from the fire and others reconstructed. Also, amongst numerous exhibits, is a rare early 17th-century astrolabe, ancient charts, the aeroplane in which the Portuguese made the first flight across the Southern Atlantic, etc. (The collections are being transferred to the Palacio das Laranjeiras, in Palma de Baixo, North Lisbon, pending the construction of a proper Museum).

Aquarium Vasco da Gama, Algés, near Lisbon. Besides an important collection of live animals, it possesses the extremely rich oceanographic collection of D. Carlos I, obtained during the various scientific expeditions of that Sovereign; and a perfect collection of about 150 models of fishing vessels.

Museum of Henrique Monfroy de Seixas (This is a private Museum, which was recently lent by the collector to the Ministry of Marine, to be included in the Maritime Museum; where it will retain its individuality, constituting a valuable record of Portuguese Naval History). This splendid collection contains several hundred models of warships from the time of the last sailing ships to the present day; fishing boats used along the whole of the Portuguese coastline; river craft; pleasure craft; and also ancient royal barges—very valuable models with gold lanterns—all of them to scale and most perfectly executed; as well as documents and thousands of photographs.

FARO (South Coast of Portugal). *Maritime Museum Admiral Ramalho Ortigão*. This annex to the Southern Maritime Department contains 68 pictures of nautical subjects; 45 models of coastal and river fishing vessels; and also fishing nets, tackle and implements, and models of naval construction, etc.

ILHAVO (North Coast of Portugal). *Municipal Museum of Ilhavo*. Occupies eleven rooms and contains a considerable maritime collection, consisting of 62 models of fishing boats; and numerous engravings, paintings, etc. Amongst the most important is an azimuthal needle that throws light on the description of the marking needle of the celebrated Portuguese navigator João de Lisboa, who wrote a navigational treatise in the beginning of the 16th Century; the same as the one in the Museum at Hamburg.

RUSSIA

LENINGRAD. As Leningrad is the only place to which a foreigner may travel in the U.S.S.R., information about other Museums in Russia is not easily obtainable. The *Naval Museum* in Leningrad is based on a periodic arrangement, starting with the models of Peter the Great's time, and through to the present day. A series of rooms is devoted to World War II; and contains models of present-day Russian ships.

SPAIN

MADRID. *Museo Naval* (Ministry of Marine). Director: Captain Don Julio Guillen. An important collection, containing numerous models, chiefly of old Spanish ships-of-war. There does not appear to be any other considerable collection of ship models in Spain.

SWEDEN

STOCKHOLM. *State Maritime Historical Museum*. Director: Gerh. Albe, Kavallerivägen, Stockholm. Contains the assembled collections of the Royal Swedish Navy, starting with those brought together at Karlskrona in the 18th Century under Admiral Chapman (1721-1805); to which have been added the maritime commercial collections, privately gathered in Stockholm after the year 1912. The whole are assembled in a magnificent new building opened by King Gustav V in 1938 and are admirably displayed. The collections include models, drawings and pictures of warships and merchantmen, forming magnificent series from early times to the present day; to which are added actual relics from various types of ships.

GÄVLE. *Gävle Museum*. Director: Dr. Ph. Humbla. The department of maritime commerce shows the development of the shipping and ship-building of the town.

GOTHENBURG. *The Maritime Museum*. Director: Captain Olof Traung. Founded by the Nautical Association of Gothenburg and now in the possession of the town. Its large collections consist of models, etc., illustrating the development of Swedish maritime commerce from the most ancient times; and ship-building, fishing, lighthouses, port organisation and oceanography are also fully represented.

HALMSTAD. *Halmstad Museum*. Director: Dr. Erik Salvén. Collections illustrative of the maritime commerce of the Halland Coast.

HELSINGBORG. *Helsingborg Museum*. Director: T. Martensson. Contains a department of maritime commerce, illustrating the shipping life through the ages.

KALMAR. *Kalmar Museum*. Director: Dr. Manne Hofrén. Collections include a large section devoted to models, pictures and original objects illustrating the maritime commerce of the town and district.

KARLSKRONA. *The Model Chamber of the Naval Dockyard*. Under the charge of the Superintendent of the Dockyard. Includes exhibits illustrating the work of the dockyard, and a large collection of figure-heads from old Swedish warships.

LIDKÖPING. *Lidköping Museum*. Director: Benjamin Lidholm. Collections illustrating the maritime commerce in the Swedish Lakes, principally Lake Vener, the Göta Canal, and the Trollhätte Canal.

UNITED STATES OF AMERICA

WASHINGTON, D.C. Naval Historical Foundation, c/o Office of Naval Records and Library, Navy Department, 25. Sponsor of Truxton-Decatur Naval Museum, Washington, D.C. A fine collection of prints, paintings, models, photographs, documents, etc. on the U.S. Navy. Truxton-Decatur Museum founded in 1948 to display selected exhibits owned by the Foundation.

United States National Museum (Smithsonian Institution). Curator: Frank Taylor, Div. of Engineering. Large watercraft collection of American types. Actual boats, half models, builders' and rigged models. Collection strong on small boat types, fishing schooners, pilot boats, with some clipper ship models. Depository of Historical American Merchant Marine Survey (WPA) plans and specifications of commercial sailing craft. A watercraft collection catalogue, published 1924.

United States Navy Department, 25. Scale and half models and other material, including fine old prints and paintings pertaining to U.S. Navy and battles. Navy Plan Collection. Paintings by World War II Navy combat artists. Majority of collection in storage, temporary and loan exhibitions held in the Navy Department buildings and elsewhere.

ANDOVER, MASS. Addison Gallery of American Art, Phillips Academy. Rigged scale models of American merchant sailing vessels, paintings, etc.

ANNAPOLIS, MD. United States Naval Academy Museum. Material pertaining to the U.S. Navy; pictures, models, flags, relics of famous American naval heroes. Houdon bust of J. P. Jones. Colonel H. H. Rogers' Collection of British Admiralty 17th- and 18th-century dockyard models, including the very important Cuckfield Park models. Other models, including early New York pilot schooners; posters, documents (Rosenbach Collection), and letters. Catalogues published.

BOSTON, MASS. Marine Museum of the old State House, State Street. Historic objects associated with Boston and New England in the development of the merchant marine and the U.S. Navy. Some fine old rigged models, etc. Strong on Boston merchant ships. Some clipper ship half models.

Museum of Fine Arts, Marine Room, Huntington Avenue and the Fenway. Several ship models and oil paintings by Robert Salmon and others, showing maritime Boston.

CAMBRIDGE, MASS. Francis Russell Hart Nautical Museum, Massachusetts Institute of Technology. (Founded 1921.) Models of famous ships, prints, whaling material, charts, plans and books. Arthur H. Clark Collection. Owen half models. Small catalogue published.

CHICAGO, ILL. Chicago Historical Society, Clark Street and North Avenue. Great Lakes material, models and pictures, some items of the Van Cleeve Collection.

Museum of Science and Industry, Jackson Park. Marine transportation in working models, display models, etc. Publishes annual reports and bulletins.

GLEN COVE, L.I., NEW YORK. Webb Institute of Naval Architecture. (Founded 1889.) A private collection of drawings, plans and half models of Isaac and William H. Webb. Ships, sail and steam.

HUNTINGTON, L.I., NEW YORK. Vanderbilt Marine Museum, Centerport. Private collection, mostly marine biology and whaling, but some maritime material including Polynesian canoes and models.

HYDE PARK, NEW YORK. Franklin D. Roosevelt Library. Models, prints, paintings, manuscripts and photographs on the U.S. Navy and merchant marine, collected by the late President.

MARIETTA, OHIO. River Museum, Campus Martius. Models, relics and pictures of steamboats, pertaining to Mississippi and Ohio Rivers. Museum established with co-operation of Sons and Daughters of Pioneer Rivermen.

MYSTIC, CONN. Marine Historical Association, Inc. Curator: Carl Cutler. A large collection of American maritime material, including rigged models, both sail and steam, prints, paintings, relics, figure-heads, Cramp half models, Brengle collection of Roux and other paintings. Some plans and good half models of American sealers and Connecticut craft. A New England 'pinky', the actual whaler *Charles W. Morgan* and the famous full-rigged school ship *Joseph Conrad* are included in a proposed reconstruction of wharves and buildings of the Greenman Shipyard. Publishes bulletins and other literature.

NANTUCKET, MASS. Nantucket Historical Association, Nantucket Island. (Founded 1894.) The maritime collection has been housed in an old candle works since 1930. Portraits, whaling pictures, prints, and gear and records of Nantucket whaling, models and relics, including model of a set of ship 'Camels.'

NEW BEDFORD, MASS. Old Dartmouth Historical Society and Bourne Whaling Museum, 37 North Water Street. (Founded 1903.) Very fine collection of material on New England whale fisheries, models, relics, whaling gear, log-books, scrimshaw and objects made and collected by American whalemen; rigged models, including an English cutter and a clipper topsail schooner. A half-size model of the barque *Laconda* is in a large hall built in 1916. Reconstructed ships. Publishes Bulletins, etc.

NEWBURYPORT, MASS. Newburyport Historical Society. Models, pictures, log-books, diaries and manuscripts of New England merchant sailing vessels and Chinese craft.

NEWPORT NEWS, VA. The Mariner's Museum. (Founded 1930.) An important, large and varied collection of maritime material of world-wide scope. Prints and paintings of seaports, sailing vessels, steamers (the Eldredge Steamship Collection including Bards, Jacobsens, etc.), half models by George Steers and others, rigged models, marine china, lighthouse and life-saving material, figure-heads, anchors, actual small watercraft and relics. Adney model Indian canoe collection. Large marine library. Publishes occasional monographs, exhibit catalogues and guides.

NEW YORK, N.Y.C. India House, 1 Hanover Square. An excellent private collection of marine prints, paintings, a few models, figure-heads and other relics, housed in a large private club. Published a fine illustrated catalogue.

Museum of the City of New York, Marine Museum Section, 1220 Fifth Avenue. Collection of paintings, prints, models and relics, including a few half models and a number of rigged models of local craft. Also a fine diorama of New York waterfront, etc. Publishes annual reports.

Museum of Science and Industry, Rockefeller Center. Marine transportation in working and display, "Model Ships of All Ages," etc.

New York Historical Society, 170 Central Park West. A marine gallery covering maritime history of the port of New York, Hudson River and Long Island Sound in prints, paintings, models and relics. Naval history collection, Murdock steamboat collection,

Bard and Jacobsen steamboat paintings. New York prints and *memorabilia*. Published New York Historical Society Quarterly.

The New York Yacht Club, 37 West 44th Street. The best private collection of half models, yachting trophies, prints and paintings pertaining to American yachting, with special emphasis on N.Y.Y.C. vessels from 1845. Rigged models, including schooner *America*.

Seamen's Bank for Savings, 74 Wall Street. Private collection, housed in the bank, of oil paintings of early American sailing ships and steamships, mostly by Jacobsen. A number of ship models.

Seamen's Church Institute, 25 South Street. Paintings, models and selected exhibits displayed, and the Conrad Memorial Library maintained, for personnel of the U.S. Merchant Marine. Monthly publication, "The Lookout".

PHILADELPHIA, PA. Franklin Institute, Hall of Marine Transportation, Parkway. Models, sail, steam and shipbuilding, showing progress of marine transport. Some rigged models of local interest. John Fitch's pioneer steamboat model submitted to American Philosophical Society. Lenthall Papers (Naval Plans, 1815-1855).

PORTLAND, MAINE. Marine Historical Society. A few half models.

PROVIDENCE, R.I. Rhode Island Historical Society. Models and pictures of Long Island Sound and Narragansett Bay maritime items, sail and steam.

SAG HARBOR, L.I., NEW YORK. Whaling Museum. Small collection of whaling material, models and whale boats, records, prints, etc. pertaining to early whaling from Long Island.

SALEM, MASS. Peabody Museum. (Founded 1867.) Curator: Lawrence Jenkins. Collection started by East India Marine Society and housed in East India Marine Hall from 1824. Merged with Peabody Institute. Very fine collection of material on Salem and New England sailing vessels. Very strong on half models of fishing vessels and Salem merchant ships. Good plan collection and large collection of marine photos. Roux paintings, Bradlee steamship collection, whaling material, ship models, nautical instruments and Bowditch records, early figure-heads, relics, etc. Also ethnological collections. Publishes occasional monographs and catalogues. Headquarters of "The American Neptune: A Quarterly Journal of Maritime History" and of the Steamship Historical Society.

Steamship Historical Society of America, Headquarters, c/o Peabody Museum. (Founded 1939). Regional chapters in New York, Boston, etc. Prints, paintings, models, photographs and relics of American steamboats and steamships owned by individual members and periodically displayed in special exhibitions held at various museums and historical societies. Publishes quarterly "Steamboat Bill of Facts" and reprints of steamboatiana.

SAN FRANCISCO, CALIF. M.H. de Young Memorial Museum, Maritime Department, Golden Gate Park, 18. Small but good collection of ship models, paintings, prints, etc.

Museum of Science and Industry (Spreckles Museum), Marine Section, Aquatic Park Center, Treasure Island. (Founded 1940.) Ship models, prints and relics pertaining to the West Coast.

SEARSPORT, MAINE. Penobscot Marine Museum. (Founded 1936.) Small but select collection of paintings by Roux and others. Models, charts, etc. pertaining to Maine sailing vessels. Occasional publications.

STATEN ISLAND, NEW YORK. New York Public Library, St. George Branch. A few models and relics. Well-rounded collection of marine books.

Sailor's Snug Harbor, West Brighton. Sail and steam merchant-ship paintings and models.

CANADA

SAINT JOHN, N.B. New Brunswick Museum, Marine Gallery. Prints, portraits, flags, relics and models of sailing ships, steamers and fishermen of maritime provinces and Bay of Fundy.